H E A L T

CHILD PROTECTION
MESSAGES FROM RESEARCH

STUDIES IN CHILD PROTECTION

LONDON: HMSO

ISBN 0 11 321781 1

All the titles in this series are available from HMSO:

Parental Perspectives in Cases of Suspected Child Abuse
Hedy Cleaver and Pam Freeman (The Dartington Team)
HMSO 1995. ISBN 0 11 321786 2 £22

Child Protection Practice: Private Risks and Public Remedies
Elaine Farmer and Morag Owen (The University of Bristol Team)
HMSO 1995. ISBN 0 11 321787 0 £25

The Prevalence of Child Sexual Abuse in Britain
Deborah Ghate and Liz Spencer (Social and Community Planning
Research)
HMSO 1995. ISBN 0 11 321783 8 £17.50

Development After Physical Abuse in Early Childhood:
A Follow-Up Study of Children on Protection Registers
Jane Gibbons Bernard Gallagher, Caroline Bell and David Gordon
(University of East Anglia)
HMSO 1995. ISBN 0 11 321790 £25

Inter-agency Coordination in Child Protection
Christine Hallett (The University of Stirling)
HMSO 1995. ISBN 0 11 321789 7 £35

Working Together in Child Protection
Elizabeth Birchall and Christine Hallett (The University of Stirling)
HMSO 1995. ISBN 0 11 321830 3 £35

Paternalism or Partnership? Family Involvement in the Child
Protection Process
June Thoburn, Ann Lewis and David Shemmings (University of East Anglia)
HMSO 1995. ISBN 0 11 321788 9 £28

Operating the Child Protection System
Jane Gibbons, Sue Conroy and Caroline Bell (University of East Anglia)
HMSO 1995. ISBN 0 11 321785 4 £14.95

I am pleased to have the opportunity to provide the foreword to this important publication which I am sure will prove to be a significant contribution to thinking and practice in child protection.

Well publicised cases of tragic suffering inflicted on children in the seventies and eighties raised public awareness of the issue of child protection. Public concern about the safety of children placed heavy responsibilities on the agencies in the front line. The way those agencies have discharged their responsibilities has itself sometimes given rise to public anxieties. A suspicion that child abuse has occurred has a traumatic effect on a family. The overriding need to protect the child while minimising damaging consequences for the family can involve agonising decisions for those working in child protection. A number of inquiries raised questions about the way agencies arrived at decisions on when to act, the nature of interventions and when to start and to stop providing services.

The Government took heed of these questions and commissioned a programme of research into child protection. That programme has now reached fruition and 20 individual studies have been completed. This document sets out the key messages arising out of those studies.

The results of the research are wide ranging and I shall not attempt to summarise them in this short foreword. Some predominant themes do, however, seem to me to emerge. Among these are:

- the way we, as a society, define abuse
- the effects of the child protection process on children and families who experience it
- side effects of interventions by child protection agencies
- the effectiveness of the process.

We must not pretend that actions taken by child protection agencies can ever guarantee that parents will not harm their children. The danger of trying to give such guarantees and of pillorying those agencies when harm does occur is that inappropriate interventions may be made out of fear. This overview supplies a context for those working in this sensitive field and examines the nature and consequences of interventions. The research evidence points towards ways in which professionals can best protect children.

Outcomes are usually better and the social work task easier when parents are involved in the process. The spirit of the *Children Act* 1989 is that there should be a balance between child protection and family support services. A significant finding of the researchers was that enquiries were too often characterised as investigations and that better outcomes might be achieved if children's needs were prioritised and matched to appropriate services. The research indicates that real benefits may arise if there is a focus on the needs of children and families rather than a narrow concentration on the alleged incident of abuse.

A major theme is the importance of training and supervision of social workers in child protection. Professionals must be experienced, knowledgeable and skilled and no amount of central or local guidance material can substitute for this. Common sense, professional judgement and good back-up for front-line staff are vital if thresholds are to be correctly judged, if parents and the wider family are to play an effective part and if extremely difficult situations are to be handled sensitively.

The research itself has a part to play in the educative process. This document is not intended as a practice text book. Lessons for practice can, however, be gleaned from it and the final section includes exercises which can be put to good use as learning material.

I urge all those working in child protection training and management to familiarise themselves with the messages coming out of the research and to assist front-line practitioners to use the research base to inform and improve their day to day practice.

John Bowis OBE MP
Parliamentary Under Secretary of State

The advisory group

This report has been prepared by members of the Dartington Social Research Unit, Roger Bullock, Michael Little, Spencer Millham and Kevin Mount with the help of an advisory group. Membership of the group reflected the range of professionals involved in supporting and protecting vulnerable children. In addition, drafts were read by the researchers whose work was reviewed, by other academics interested in this field and by policy makers, trainers and practitioners. The successful completion of the research programme was achieved as a result of the commitment of many people. In particular, the authors would like to express their appreciation to the Department of Health for its essential support and to Carolyn Davies, Wendy Rose, Rupert Hughes, Kathleen Taylor and Rosemary Arkley for managing and co-ordinating the whole initiative. Members of the advisory group were:

Rosemary Arkley	Social Services Inspector, Department of Health
Celia Atherton	Co-Director, Family Rights Group
David Behan	Director of Social Services, Cleveland
Sue Botes	Professional Officer, Health Visitors Association
Eric Bowker	Child Protection Policy Desk, Metropolitan Police
Chris Brannan	Consumer Services Manager, Shropshire Social Services
Carolyn Davies	Senior Principal Research Liaison Officer, Department of Health
Cathy Doran	Services Manager, Haringey Social Services
Keith Driver	Obscene Publications Department, Metropolitan Police
Elizabeth Fradd	Nursing Division, Department of Health
Breeda Gallagher	Senior Clinical Nursing Officer, Leeds Community and Mental Health Services, NHS Trust
Jane Gibbons	Senior Research Fellow, Social Work Development Unit, University of East Anglia
Geoff Gildersleeve	Assistant Director, Norfolk Social Services
Christopher Hobbs	Consultant Community Paediatrician, St James Hospital, Leeds
Rupert Hughes	Assistant Secretary, Department of Health
Peter Jeffries	Assistant Chief Probation Officer, Inner London Probation Service

David Jones	Consultant Child Psychiatrist, The Park Hospital for Children, Oxford
Ravi Kohli	Senior Lecturer in Social Work, Middlesex University
Zarrina Kurtz	Regional Consultant in Public Health Medicine, South West Thames RHA
Felicity Leenders	Nursing Division, Department of Health
Jeremy Lissamore	Senior Medical Officer, Department of Health
Angela Mukhopadhay	Education Inspector, OFSTED
Georgina Robinson	Children's Services Officer, Gloucestershire Social Services
Wendy Rose	Assistant Chief Inspector, Department of Health
Jane Scott	Development Officer, Dartington Social Research Unit
Sue Shepherd	Medical Division, Department of Health
Jane Sloan	Social Work Consultant, Cornwall Social Services
Marjorie Smith	Deputy Director, Thomas Coram Research Unit
Mike Stein	Senior Lecturer, Continuing Education Department, Leeds University
Kathleen Taylor	Child Protection Policy, Community Service Division, Department of Health
June Thoburn	Professor of Social Work, University of East Anglia

Contents

Introduction

This publication is the third concerned with summarising and disseminating the results of child-care research funded by the Department of Health. Like its predecessors, *Social Work Decisions in Child Care* (1985) and *Patterns and Outcomes in Child Placement* (1991), it seeks to make research findings accessible to professionals working with children and to demonstrate the relevance of these results for policy and practice.

The focus of the previous two volumes was children looked after away from home. This publication is concerned with child protection and child abuse. As before, it is hoped that key messages from 20 recently completed studies will be conveyed to practitioners, managers, students, Area Child Protection Committee members, indeed to all working with children and families.

The need for new information became manifest in the 1980s after a series of child abuse scandals. The Cleveland Inquiry in 1987, chaired by Lady Justice Butler-Schloss, followed public concern about the removal from home of children suspected of being sexually abused. Had professionals been over-zealous, had parents' rights been disregarded? The Inquiry gave a new salience to the problem of child sexual abuse and raised important questions about the ways in which child welfare agencies handle cases coming to their notice. The following gaps in knowledge were identified:

- the definition and diagnosis of child maltreatment
- the response of protection agencies when suspected abuse comes to light
- the most effective forms of intervention.

These raised important practice questions, namely; when to take action, how to intervene, when to remove children and when and how to withdraw services.

As part of a Government response to the problems raised by Cleveland and other inquiries, the Department of Health initiated a programme of research studies into child protection. This included child sexual abuse but looked more broadly to include physical maltreatment and neglect. Naturally, in developing the programme, contemporary policy issues were influential. The *Children Act 1989* was soon to be implemented and some revision of the 1988 guidance, *Working Together,* was envisaged. There was also a body of research knowledge from this country and abroad relevant to some of the problems.

The issues identified as being in need of further scrutiny have all been covered by the research programme, although the emphasis on some areas has been greater than on others. Studies have explored control within the family, co-ordination of services, parental experience of enquiries, stress on social workers, whether children should be supported at home, treatment approaches and long-term outcomes.

The book begins with an Overview which seeks to summarise and bring together the findings from the 20 studies and overviews listed on pages 9 and 10. In such an exercise three main areas of interest emerge. Firstly, there is an attempt to define abuse in the context of normal childhood experience and to estimate the incidence of different types of maltreatment in society. Secondly, the book attempts to identify who gets caught up in the child protection process and how children's safety is achieved. Thirdly, it focuses on what conclusions can be drawn in relation to good practice, from the days of the first enquiry to situations where a child is removed from home and receives treatment.

Because the book is based on a particular research programme it inevitably reflects some concerns more than others. Evidence relevant to legislation, inspection and guidance is more forthcoming than are clinical results of treatment interventions or findings pertinent to criminal and family law. It is also the case that important groups, such as children with disabilities, those placed for adoption or those living in residential or specialist foster care, are not specifically dealt with. Similarly, issues of race, gender and rights may not be as salient in the studies as some readers might wish, neither is there much on the perpetrators of abuse. Some of these issues are addressed in other projects, including those subsequently commissioned by the Department of Health.

In the light of these observations, it is important to stress what this publication cannot provide. It is not a text book or practice guide which tells professionals what to do with individual cases; but it should nevertheless inform the planning and delivery of services. Neither is it a statement of best policies with regard to child protection; but it does explain how society's response to maltreatment has changed over time. It is not a research document with methodological discussions and comprehensive references to justify statements, but it does offer ways in which practitioners can see if the results are true for their particular areas of work and directs readers to other sources of information likely to be useful.

The structure of the book will be familiar to those who have used *Social Work Decisions in Child Care* and *Patterns and Outcomes in Child Placement*. It begins with an *Overview* which seeks to bring together the principal messages of all 20 reports and to produce observations and findings which are not immediately apparent from reading each study in turn. The second section consists of short *summaries* of each project. The third part provides exercises for practitioners to see if the findings are *'true for us'*, thus answering frequent criticisms of child-care research, such as 'it might have been true then, but it's not true now' or 'it may be true there, but it's not the case here!'

The Overview has been written to be read from beginning to end. Other information, such as short answers to questions frequently posed by practitioners, have been interspersed to encourage readers to make use of the full research reports. However the book is used, the aim is to inform everyone working in the child protection field and ultimately to enhance the welfare of children.

The Department of Health funded studies reviewed are:

WORKING TOGETHER IN CHILD PROTECTION
Elizabeth Birchall and Christine Hallett (University of Stirling)
HMSO, 1995

PARENTAL PERSPECTIVES IN CASES OF SUSPECTED CHILD ABUSE
Hedy Cleaver and Pam Freeman (The Dartington Team)
HMSO, 1995

CHILD PROTECTION PRACTICE: PRIVATE RISKS AND PUBLIC REMEDIES
DECISION MAKING, INTERVENTION AND OUTCOME IN CHILD PROTECTION WORK
Elaine Farmer and Morag Owen (The University of Bristol Team)
HMSO, 1995

THE PREVALENCE OF CHILD SEXUAL ABUSE IN BRITAIN: A FEASIBILITY STUDY FOR A
LARGE SCALE NATIONAL SURVEY OF THE GENERAL POPULATION
Deborah Ghate and Liz Spencer (Social and Community Planning Research)
HMSO, 1995

DEVELOPMENT AFTER PHYSICAL ABUSE IN EARLY CHILDHOOD: A FOLLOW-UP STUDY
OF CHILDREN ON PROTECTION REGISTERS
Jane Gibbons, Bernard Gallagher, Caroline Bell and David Gordon (University
of East Anglia)
HMSO, 1995

OPERATING THE CHILD PROTECTION SYSTEM: A STUDY OF CHILD PROTECTION
PRACTICES IN ENGLISH LOCAL AUTHORITIES
Jane Gibbons, Sue Conroy and Caroline Bell (University of East Anglia)
HMSO, 1995

INTER-AGENCY COORDINATION IN CHILD PROTECTION
Christine Hallett (University of Stirling)
HMSO, 1995

THE EXTENT AND NATURE OF ORGANISED AND RITUAL SEXUAL ABUSE: RESEARCH
FINDINGS
Jean La Fontaine (London School of Economics)
HMSO, 1994

SEXUALLY ABUSED CHILDREN AND ADOLESCENTS AND YOUNG PERPETRATORS OF
SEXUAL ABUSE WHO WERE TREATED IN VOLUNTARY COMMUNITY FACILITIES
Elizabeth Monck and Michelle New (Institute of Child Health, University of
London)
HMSO, 1995

CHILD SEXUAL ABUSE: A DESCRIPTIVE AND TREATMENT STUDY
Elizabeth Monck, Elaine Sharland, Arnon Bentovim, Gillian Goodall, Caroline
Hyde and Rebekah Lwin (Institute of Child Health, University of London)
HMSO, 1995

PROFESSIONAL INTERVENTION IN CHILD SEXUAL ABUSE
Elaine Sharland, David Jones, Jane Aldgate, Hilary Seal and Margaret Croucher
(The University of Oxford Team)
HMSO, 1995

NORMAL FAMILY SEXUALITY AND SEXUAL KNOWLEDGE IN CHILDREN
Marjorie Smith and Margaret Grocke
Royal College of Psychiatrists/Gorkill Press, 1995

PARENTAL CONTROL WITHIN THE FAMILY: THE NATURE AND EXTENT OF PARENTAL
VIOLENCE TO CHILDREN
Marjorie Smith, Penney Bee, Andrea Heverin and Gavin Nobes (Thomas
Coram Research Unit team), 1995
Papers forthcoming: enquiries to Thomas Coram Research Unit, Tel. 0171-612-6957

PATERNALISM OR PARTNERSHIP? FAMILY INVOLVEMENT IN THE CHILD PROTECTION
PROCESS
June Thoburn, Ann Lewis and David Shemmings (University of East Anglia)
HMSO, 1995

In addition, the following related projects have been included:

AN EXPLORATORY STUDY OF THE PREVALENCE OF SEXUAL ABUSE IN A SAMPLE OF
16-21 YEAR OLDS
Liz Kelly, Linda Regan and Sheila Burton, Child and Woman Abuse Studies
Unit, University of North London, 1991

CHILD SEXUAL ABUSE IN NORTHERN IRELAND: A RESEARCH STUDY OF INCIDENCE
The Research Team (Queen's University, Belfast)
Greystone, 1990

EVALUATING PARENTING IN CHILD PHYSICAL ABUSE
Lorraine Waterhouse, Tom Pitcairn, Janice McGhee, Jenny Secker and Cathleen
Sullivan in *Child Abuse and Child Abusers*, Jessica Kingsley, 1993

It is hoped that the findings highlighted in this report will lead readers to consult
the texts in full. Three other reviews of the research literature might usefully be
read in conjunction with this publication:

CHILD ABUSE INTERVENTIONS: A REVIEW OF THE RESEARCH LITERATURE
David Gough
HMSO, 1993

COORDINATION AND CHILD PROTECTION
Christine Hallett and Elizabeth Birchall
HMSO, 1992

and from the United States
UNDERSTANDING CHILD ABUSE AND NEGLECT
National Research Council
National Academy Press, 1993

The problems of definition

Any discussion of child abuse and child protection services will benefit from agreements about definition. Unfortunately, there is no absolute definition of abuse. If, from a list of behaviours, ticks could be put against those which are abusive and crosses against those which are not, the task of practitioners and researchers would be made easier. In this list, hitting children might be ticked, indicating that such behaviour is abusive. But some might argue that in certain contexts it is good for children to be hit and, as at least 90% of children have this experience at some time, the behaviour could be said to be 'normal'. The tick might be replaced by a cross or, at best, by a question mark.

There are many definitions of abuse in the legal and scientific literature. Most describe abusive *incidents*, especially beating, sexual interference and neglect of children. But policy makers, researchers and practitioners are likely to consider the *context* in which such incidents occur before they will define them as abusive, a perspective that has been defined as phenomenological. The Department of Health publication, *Protecting Children: A Guide for Social Workers Undertaking a Comprehensive Assessment* (known as the 'Orange Book') is helpful in highlighting the circumstances surrounding maltreatment. A weakness of this approach, however, is one of tautology: behaviour becomes abusive as soon as practitioners describe it as such. The researchers have helped with definitions of abuse by providing evidence on what normally happens in families and what are the long-term *outcomes* of different parenting styles. Such information, in combination with data on other harmful experiences, leads to a perspective on child abuse (as opposed to a definition of child abuse) which emphasises the needs of children and the context in which maltreatment occurs.

Whatever approach is employed, it is important to reflect on what is considered abusive to children because this will determine whether, when and how to intervene. If professionals are certain that they are faced with a severe incident, in which there are no mitigating circumstances and which, left unchecked, will lead to significant harm, they have a duty to protect the child. In some situations, the authority of the court will be required, for example when an emergency protection order is needed. In other circumstances, it may be concluded that no abuse has occurred and that no action to protect the child or support the family is necessary. But most cases that come to the notice of agencies involved in child protection fall between these extremes. They very often concern children in need of support from outside the family as well as protection. Deciding whether child abuse has occurred in these – the most common – cases is difficult and forms the beginning of this discussion.

The first question is, what happens ordinarily in families?

Normal behaviour within families

Although maltreatment can occur in a variety of settings, the evidence on normal behaviour within families is important in defining what is abnormal or abusive. But even this approach has its difficulties. For example, what might be thought of as 'normal' in one generation is often 'abnormal' in another and what might be thought of as 'normal' in one social context can be 'abnormal' in another. Sending eight year olds to boarding school has been acceptable to many generations of parents in certain social classes but is considered neglectful by others. In addition, behaviour which is thought to be 'normal' because it is exhibited by the majority of parents is not necessarily 'optimal'. Most parents resort on occasions to hitting their children but many accept that it is not an effective or enduring means of control.

Nonetheless, by examining what typically happens in families, some light can be shed on the way a society decides what is abnormal. Both behaviour within families towards children – what some have described as parenting styles – and society's perspectives on what is good or bad for children change over time. No doubt, the one influences the other. Certainly the Victorian affection for the maxim 'spare the rod and spoil the child' was reflected in child rearing practices of the day, just as current attitudes towards young people are manifest in legislation and guidance.

So what are normal patterns of parenting behaviour? Most parents hit their sons and daughters, even babies in nappies. The Newsons' survey in the 1960s found that 95% of parents hit their children and that 80% of them thought it was right to do so. When they repeated the survey in the 1990s these proportions had fallen; four-fifths (81%) of parents now hit their children but half thought they should not. Marjorie Smith and colleagues at the Thomas Coram Research Unit also found that most of the 403 children they surveyed had been hit. The overall rate was 91% and three-quarters of children under the age of one had been so disciplined.

In an earlier study at the Institute of Child Health, Smith and Grocke looked at patterns of sexual behaviour within English homes. Their findings expose the gap between popular images of family life and what is actually occurring. Child protection professionals used to dealing with extremes of human behaviour tend to overestimate the levels of problem behaviour and sometimes misinterpret what is perfectly normal. To illustrate the gap between image and reality, consider the following list of behaviours and situations and try to estimate what proportion occurred within the families studied. (It might be helpful to know that the researchers focused on a random sample of children aged between four and 16 who had not been abused.)

THERE ARE ALMOST as many definitions of child abuse as there are books on the subject. The following are selected to illustrate some indication of the difficulties of reaching agreement.

The Oxford English Dictionary defines child abuse: as 'maltreatment of a child, especially by beating, sexual interference or neglect'.

The legal definition of child abuse is set down by the *Children Act,* 1989. The primary justification for the state to initiate proceedings seeking compulsory powers is actual or likely harm to the child, where harm includes both ill-treatment (which includes sexual abuse and non-physical ill-treatment such as emotional abuse) and the impairment of health or development, health meaning physical or mental health, and development meaning physical, intellectual, emotional, social, or behavioural development.

Physical abuse: 'Physical abuse implies physically harmful action directed against a child; it is usually defined by any inflicted injury such as bruises, burns, head injuries, fractures, abdominal injuries, or poisoning'. Kempe, C., Silverman, F., Steele, B., Droegmueller, W., Silver, H.

Sexual abuse: 'Sexual abuse is defined as the involvement of dependent, developmentally immature children and adolescents in sexual activities that they do not fully comprehend and to which they are unable to give informed consent or that violate the social taboos of family roles'. Schechter, M. and Roberge, L.

Parents report the child definitely or probably as having:

A touched mother's breasts
B touched father's genitalia
C drawn genitalia
D been seen masturbating
E seen 'simulated' sexual intercourse on films or TV
F seen pornographic material
G seen horror movies
H bathed with parents

H	77%
G	30%
F	9%
E	31%
D	67%
C	35%
B	12%
A	63%

These results are presented in this way to encourage reflection on how abuse is defined and what behaviours are potentially abusive. Overtly sexualised behaviour, such as excessive masturbation, sexual curiosity or touching genitals are sometimes thought of as indicators of abuse. However, the Institute of Child Health study shows that such behaviours frequently occur in moderation in the homes of 'normal' English families and that they are not *in themselves* sufficient to suggest abuse. More important is the context in which the behaviour occurs: where it takes place; who else is present; what parents think about it; the age of the child.

The difficulties of interpretation can be illustrated with the example of nakedness within families – a reasonably good indicator of parenting style. As the preceding exercise shows, it is not unusual for children to see their parents naked. But Smith and Grocke also found that the behaviour declined with age, for instance bathing with parents reduced considerably after the child's fifth birthday and did not occur post-puberty. Family type was also shown to be important; nakedness was more likely to occur in households which included both biological parents and among professional classes. The reduction in nakedness in the family is usually a natural process; parents start to cover themselves up when the children get embarrassed and bathing together becomes impractical as children get older and bigger. Again, understanding the context helps with an understanding of what is abusive. A parent walking naked before his or her children is not being abusive but if the same behaviour was occurring against the child's wishes, some maltreatment might be said to be taking place.

Does a combination of sexual behaviours indicate possible abuse? Probably not, since there is a natural association between different actions. A child who bathes with a parent is more likely to touch the parent's genitalia. Neither of these behaviours singly or in combination is a reliable sign of maltreatment. There was a small but significant group in the Institute of Child Health sample who had seen a sexually explicit video or who had witnessed sexual intercourse and, as a result, were likely to have greater sexual knowledge than their peers. In the context of an investigation this might give rise to suspicions of sexual abuse. Such a loss of innocence could be undesirable, but it would be presumptuous to call it abusive.

While it is relatively easy to chart patterns of punishment in families, these too prove inadequate indicators of abuse. Indeed, the Thomas Coram team observed that while factors previously found to be associated with physical maltreatment - such as mother's young age or children born in close sequence - were mild predictors of frequent or severe punishment, other factors more indicative of daily life stress were stronger. Parents hit their children when they could not cope with minor difficulties, such as the child's own behaviour or disputes between siblings. Any practitioner knows that a lot can be done to improve the situation of these families - for example by providing general support to raise parents' irritation threshold and specific advice such as how to handle sibling aggression. Punishment can be abusive but it should not be the only focus of child protection interventions. Equally important is support for children and families in need.

Thresholds for intervention

It should be clear from this evidence that child abuse is not an absolute concept. Most behaviour has to be seen in context before it can be thought of as maltreatment. With the exception of some sexual abuse, it should also be clear that maltreatment is seldom an event, a single incident that requires action to protect the child. Some forms of parenting styles and ways of bringing up children are abusive - or at least potentially abusive. Maltreatment viewed in this way is unlikely to be just physical abuse or emotional abuse. Types of abuse overlap so that a child who has been physically maltreated will almost certainly have suffered emotionally, and sexual abuse may involve physical force or threat of punishment.

THE ASSOCIATION between types of abuse is illustrated in Farmer and Owen's study. They found that the existence of secondary concerns was a factor significantly related to the placement of a child's name on the protection register.

In one-third of cases where the main concern was *neglect,* there were also concerns about *physical abuse*.

In one-fifth of cases where the main concern was *physical abuse*, there were also concerns about *neglect*.

In one-quarter of cases where the main concern was *sexual abuse*, there were also concerns about *neglect*.

In one-sixth of cases where the main concern was *sexual abuse* there were also concerns about *physical abuse*.

In one-quarter of cases where the main concern was *physical abuse*, there were also concerns about *emotional abuse*.

If the focus is to be on events in context and the combination of types of maltreatment that can occur, how do professionals judge that a child is being abused? Some plurality will be necessary as no single definition of abuse is likely to satisfy all the different parties - the policy maker deciding where to place scarce resources, the public worrying about how best to bring up children, the social scientist trying to estimate how much abuse exists and the professional making difficult judgements about child safety.

This complex situation is clarified by introducing the idea of a continuum of abuse. Several research teams concluded that abuse was better understood if the focus of concern was on behaviour which children ordinarily encountered but which in certain circumstances could be defined as maltreatment. Once this step has been taken, questions for researchers and practitioners tend to be about chronicity and severity of behaviours, such as how much shouting at children can be said to be harmful. This perspective is certainly an antidote to the idea introduced at the beginning where specific behaviour is defined as either acceptable or unacceptable. Gil's finding that physical abuse was often discipline gone too far is a good illustration of the continuum model. The studies by Marjorie Smith of normal family life found that most incidents that cause concern can be understood in this way but there are important exceptions. Dropping a baby on to a bed, for example, rests between gentle play at one end of a continuum and extreme frenzy at the other; pulling out fingernails can only be described as abusive.

Professionals see parenting behaviour on a continuum but they have the additional duty to decide whether to intervene and, if so, how. To do this they must draw a threshold; this involves deciding both the point beyond which a behaviour (or parenting style) can be considered maltreatment and the point beyond which it becomes necessary for the state to take action. Hence, decisions about what is abusive are closely tied to decisions about whether the state should intervene. Child protection professionals make many of these decisions on behalf of society. As later sections will show, thresholds placed at different stages of the child protection process determine the way a case progresses; for example, the decision to alert parents, to call a case conference or to add a name to the protection register.

As the following diagram illustrates, the amount of abuse in society depends upon the point at which thresholds are drawn. Move the dividing line upwards and the amount of abuse in society diminishes; a downward movement has the opposite effect. Viewed in this way it can be seen how, even when parenting styles remain the same over time, the amount of abuse uncovered by child protection agencies may increase or decrease depending on the drawing of the threshold.

A look at changes over the last century would suggest that the threshold beyond which child abuse is considered to occur is gradually being lowered. This is happening for a variety of reasons, including an emphasis on the rights of children as individuals, ease of disclosures, the influence of feminist social theories about victimisation and public expectation that the state should intervene in the privacy of family life. Society continually reconstructs definitions of maltreatment which sanction intervention; in 1871 the concern was abuse by adoptive parents; in 1885 it was teenage prostitution; in 1908 incest; then, later, neglect, physical abuse, sexual and emotional abuse. The state remains selective in its concerns and there is a difference between behaviour known to be harmful to children and behaviour which attracts the attention of child protection practitioners. For example, professionals' interest in school bullying is perhaps not as great as parents and children would wish it to be and domestic violence is only just beginning to achieve salience as a cause of concern. Jane Gibbons helpfully summarises the situation when she says that 'as a phenomenon, child maltreatment is more like pornography than whooping cough. It is a socially constructed phenomenon which reflects values and opinions of a particular culture at a particular time'.

HOW IS GATE-KEEPING achieved in the child protection process?

Most of the researchers found the idea of a threshold to be the best way of understanding gate-keeping at different stages in the child protection process.

Thresholds determine the key 'when' questions facing professionals: when to define something as abusive, when to intervene, when to confront or raise the issue with parents, when to call a protection conference and when to remove a child.

Several thresholds exist. Some are clear and unequivocal but others depend on context and cultural values.

The placing of the threshold is influenced by moral and legal questions, pragmatic concerns and, recently, outcome evidence and the concerns of parents and children. There are pressures for stronger gate-keeping, such as when parents feel that their rights have been ignored by high-handed professionals, and for opening the door further, for example to include bullying and racial attacks.

Once acceptable definitions of abuse have been reached, the threshold for concern is clear; the *Children Act* 1989 and *Working Together* specify that *all* reports and suspicions of child abuse must be taken seriously and assessed. Subsequent gate-keeping is more negotiable. In deciding to move from assessment to enquiry there may be long-term benefits for children and families if potentially abusive incidents or situations are viewed in a broad context. This leads to a focus on wider needs in which there is a protection issue.

If this perspective on child abuse holds, what are the influences on the thresholds which separate non-intervention from intervention? Nearly all the research teams provided evidence on this issue and four dimensions were found to be important. Initially, there is a moral aspect, fundamental to any legislation. Over time, moral concerns change and policy makers add, subtract and amend categories of abuse; witness the recent inclusion of sexual abuse and the dropping of grave concern as a separate category from *Working Together* in 1991.

Professionals, in addition to observing procedural rules, also make a number of pragmatic judgements related to whether interventions will help. Such assessments should consider the whole situation and the interventions applied will take account of potential behaviours and responses in their wider context. Ideally, professionals assess the severity and duration of the suspected abuse; they consider the child's reaction and his or her perceptions; they look at the parents' attitude and willingness to co-operate; and they sometimes think about the effects upon the child's development. Ideally, they look for any protective factors for the child, something that will make his or her life more viable. Professionals also have to weigh up the effects of the intervention on the child's long-term well-being.

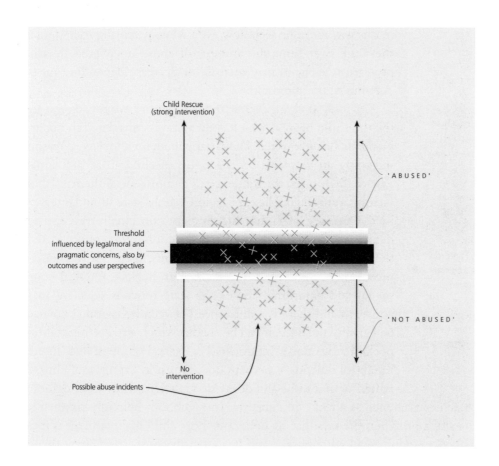

IN THIS OVERVIEW, there are frequent references to 'family' and 'parents'. Because of the changing structure of the family in modern society and the fragmentation found in many abuse situations these terms need defining for each case. It was found that some 'families' in which abuse had occurred were lone mothers with a single child while others were multi-generational and involved wider kin. Although researchers were sensitive to this issue it was frequently easier to interview mothers in the studies than fathers, other relatives or resident partners and this needs to be borne in mind when interpreting results.

The research teams also drew attention to important dimensions sometimes missing from assessments. Although procedures are constantly developing, child protection professionals remain tardy in using evidence about the effects of a behaviour or parenting style on outcomes for the child. Deborah Ghate and Liz Spencer in their feasibility study of the prevalence of sexual abuse found it unhelpful to refer to 'cases of abuse' without understanding the long-term effects. Does hitting a child once do any emotional damage? Can children who have been sexually abused make a recovery? This perspective defines a behaviour or way of upbringing as abusive only when it is debilitating for the child. It makes a distinction between abusive action - what carers do - and harm - the impact on the child.

Many of the researchers attest to the benefits of parental participation in decisions involving children. Just as it can be worthwhile listening to family members' views about how best to protect the child, taking account of parents' and children's perspectives of what constitutes abuse is vital. Parents tend to worry not only about external influences upon their children's well-being, particularly racial abuse or horror movies on television or video, but also environmental hazards such as the danger from busy main roads or unsuitable play spaces. Children worry about interpersonal relationships, particularly if they are unhappy at school, and yet these sources of potential harm are seldom part of professionals' reckoning.

Thus there are several influences upon the drawing of the threshold for defining abuse and sanctioning appropriate action. At the time the research was conducted, the most important of these influences were: *moral/legal* questions and the *pragmatic* concerns of professionals. The researchers also concluded that *outcome* evidence and *parent/child* concerns should play a greater role in professional decisions about what is and what is not abusive.

Occasionally the movement of the threshold and pressures for change become evident. The Cleveland Inquiry in 1987 caused much soul-searching about the state's response to suspicions of sexual maltreatment of children by parents. Particularly evident were moral concerns about levels of sexual abuse within our society, the practicalities of intervening with victims and the perspectives of parents who felt their rights had been scanted by high-handed professionals and the precipitate removal of their offspring. Missing from the discussion was any reliable outcome evidence, for example, about the effects of sexual abuse or the consequences of taking emergency action to remove a child from home. Certain influences on the threshold, such as the weight of moral concern, were tending to force the threshold downwards, urging professionals to intervene with more children. Other influences were working in the opposite direction, not least the argument that society had become over-zealous and that efforts to protect children were frequently counter-productive.

Influences on the thresholds for intervention are frequently linked. It is noticeable that most moral concerns about children centre on the child's life within the family household. Discussions about the practicalities of intervening in the home inevitably follow, leading to debate about the balance between parents' and children's rights and to research into what happens to children maltreated by relatives. This situation can be seen in the dilemma faced by child protection services with regard to domestic violence and the scientific debate about the role of men in many cases of child maltreatment.

On the other hand, societal trends may pull professional concern in another direction, away from the context of the family home. Empirical evidence about the effects of bullying in school, for example, has raised questions about the protection of children outside the home. Even so, it is important to remember that nearly all child protection enquiries still start with questions of parental maltreatment or neglect. Cases involving abusers outside the family may achieve greater publicity but, as the study on intervention by Sharland and colleagues shows, children sexually abused by such perpetrators are the least likely to have their needs met.

AS LATER SECTIONS illustrate, teasing out the various effects of abuse and of interventions by professionals is complicated. There are the direct effects of maltreatment to consider. In addition, there are indirect effects, for example, physical injury associated with suspected child sexual abuse. The consequences of maltreatment are also manifold. For example, in sexual abuse, the pain of disclosure has to be separated from the treatment process. In the majority of physical abuse and neglect cases, poor handling of suspicion by professionals can adversely affect family functioning and subsequent support may be serving several functions in addition to protecting the child.

What is bad for children?

The evidence from the research programme illustrates the influence of known outcomes for children on the drawing of the threshold just described. In assessing the long-term effects of different parenting styles, the severity and endurance of particular incidents can be important. In a warm, supportive environment, children who have been hit once or twice seldom suffer long-term negative effects. Similarly, while a short period of neglect or emotional abuse is likely to cause children unhappiness and some harm, an important part of the professional task will be to understand the wider family context. With the exception of many child sexual abuse investigations, most professionals find themselves judging the severity and chronicity of experiences against the backdrop of other happenings in the child's life. It will also be seen that the research studies found single abusive events rarely to be the subject of Section 47 enquiries.

Long-term difficulty for children is caused in several, sometimes unexpected ways. Waterhouse, for example, in cases of physical abuse found under-control to be as much a problem as over-control in the families she studied. Parents under pressure seldom had much time for their children and were apt to lash out in a rage at the frustrations of everyday interaction. Waterhouse also emphasised the damaging effects of long-term family violence and that children regularly seeing their mother beaten can suffer as much as if they themselves had been frequently and severely hit. In contrast, in cases of marital breakdown, the conflict is rarely perceived as abusive to children even though it causes much unhappiness and may cause long-term emotional harm.

A SUMMARY OF RESEARCH, resting on such a wide range of sources and covering such a range of issues, must draw out broad themes. General principles and ideas emerge which apply to the majority of cases but not all. Many of the researchers stressed that instances of child sexual abuse did not always conform to general findings about child protection. The following points which set out ways in which sexual maltreatment differs from other types of abuse therefore need to be borne in mind.

It is found that, in most contexts, single instances of maltreatment seldom warrant much concern on the part of professionals. It is the chronicity and severity of maltreatment that influence a willingness to intervene. This is not always true of child sexual abuse, as a relatively minor, one-off event can sometimes be damaging to children and may require a strong response from protection agencies.

Generally, it is difficult to define child abuse and there are no absolute criteria on which to rely. However, compared to physical maltreatment or neglect, the thresholds which define when sexual abuse has occurred are relatively clear. There is also more parental agreement over when a sexual act can be said to be abusive.

All the researchers agreed that while a behaviour in one context will be defined as maltreatment, the same behaviour in another context would not. This rule is less easy to apply in cases of sexual abuse. Much child protection work is principally concerned with problems within the family (although child maltreatment in other contexts, for example bullying in school, is a major worry to parents). In cases of child sexual abuse, outside perpetrators and maltreatment by 'known others' like neighbours or distant relatives is more likely to feature in professional enquiries.

In other respects, the messages of the research tend to apply across the various categories of abuse. For example, most victims of child sexual abuse continue to live at home and most of those who are separated are swiftly reunited with relatives; the handling of the suspicion is as important in cases of sexual abuse as it is in other types of maltreatment; and the wider needs of families on the receiving end of a sexual abuse enquiry need to be borne in mind, particularly the psychiatric support that parents frequently request.

Although they differ in the detail of their results, those researchers that looked at the issue agree that long-term problems occur when the *parenting style* fails to compensate for the inevitable deficiencies that become manifest in the course of the 20 years or so it takes to bring up a child. During this period, occasional neglect, unnecessary or severe punishment or some form of family discord can be expected. It is a question of balance in the interactions with the child. If parenting is entirely negative, it will be damaging; if negative events are interspersed with positive experiences, outcomes may be better. In a warm supportive home, it may be better for a parent to get very cross with an errant child and later apologise than to do nothing at all. However, in families *low on warmth and high on criticism,* negative incidents accumulate as if to remind a child that he or she is unloved.

This pattern of low warmth, high criticism has been noted by several researchers. Thoburn and colleagues describe this context as one of 'emotional neglect', others prefer 'emotional maltreatment'. These terms are to be distinguished from categories of abuse, such as those listed in *Working Together.* Whatever expression is used, all of the researchers are trying to capture those contexts which are potentially harmful and generally inauspicious for children and which also place them at a higher risk of experiencing specifically abusive events, such as physical harm or even sexual maltreatment.

In these families, although parents behave badly or are unavailable to their children, they seldom – if ever – commit acts of deliberate cruelty. However, punishment, physical neglect and, very occasionally, sexual abuse are probably more likely to occur to children in low warmth, high criticism situations. There are chains of cause and effect in these families which can sometimes explain parents' maladaptive behaviour. An alcoholic father may drive a family into poverty, making a mother's task extremely difficult or a violent partner might force the rest of the family to flee to poor or overcrowded housing. Alternatively, some emotional neglect might be explained by a mother's depression. However, it is important to emphasise that households under pressure – including many disordered, reconstituted and poor families – are frequently warm and loving places in which to bring up children.

Putting to one side the severe cases, for those children who suffer from a short period of emotional neglect, the child protection process may not be the best way of meeting their needs. If, however, the family problems endure, some external support will be required, otherwise the health and development of the child will be significantly impaired. These are clearly children 'in need' as defined by the *Children Act*, 1989. In some cases, the severity of individual incidents, the long duration of poor parenting styles or the denial of abuse will result in the child suffering significant harm and stronger protection strategies will be required from the child protection process. There are, in addition, a small proportion of cases in which the abuse is extreme and cannot be explained by contextual factors; swift action to protect and possibly remove the child will be necessary.

As the following sections reveal, the research shows that many of the services provided by child care agencies - including those offered with the intent of protecting the child - alleviate the pressures on the family, reduce emotional neglect by parents and so diminish the likelihood of long-term impairment or even significant harm. These services can increase the warmth and lower the criticism experienced by the child. Unfortunately, beneficial effects are often reduced because of a preoccupation with abusive events rather than with the processes that underlie them.

A consequence of moving the threshold

Even in the absence of any behavioural change from generation to generation, it is possible by moving thresholds for society to discover new 'types' of abuse. Increasing understanding of family life has led to recognition of the damaging effects first of neglect, then physical abuse, then sexual abuse and, more recently, emotional maltreatment. More abuse and abuse categories have been identified by the successive adjustments of thresholds of intervention. Lately, paedophile rings, female perpetrators and abusing adolescents have become the focus of much concern.

The tenor of the previous discussion on parenting styles suggests that 'discoveries' of new forms of abuse need to be treated with caution as the studies by Gallagher and La Fontaine reveal. They showed that sexual abuse was sometimes organised, so that several cases coming to the notice of child protection agencies might be linked. Connections between cases occur vertically - through several generations of the same family - or horizontally - between families. Protection agencies found it difficult to handle geographical, temporal and organisational distance between cases in an abuse network and sometimes missed important connections.

PARENTS WORRY ABOUT methods of controlling their children. As earlier pages testify, most parents hit their offspring but the evidence from Smith and colleagues would suggest that few do so wantonly. The following quotations collected by the Thomas Coram team from mothers whose parenting would excite little interest on the part of child protection professionals, illustrate this point.

'A smack once is all it takes to let them know we're not gonna put up with it. Any more is excessive and unnecessary.'

'I don't smack them when they're little, it's more my fault than theirs.'

'Smacking does nothing whatsoever, they just forget about it. It just makes me feel worse.'

THE FAMILY CIRCUMSTANCES of children who are subject to a Section 47 enquiry are varied but generally sad. Cleaver and Freeman identified five types of family which help to illustrate the range of background factors which might be borne in mind when abuse is suspected.

Multi-problem families (43%) were well known to social services and displayed a wide range of difficulties. The adults in these families were highly likely to have suffered abuse themselves as children.

Specific problem families (21%) came to notice because of a particular suspicion. Such families had rarely been the recipients of welfare interventions or police concern. Ostensibly, they lived ordered lives and crossed class boundaries.

Acutely distressed families (13%) shared many of the characteristics of the first group but were distinct in the degree and frequency of accidents, misfortune and trauma they experienced. Parents could not cope, a breakdown occurred which resulted in abuse, usually physical maltreatment or neglect.

Infiltrating perpetrators (9%) affected a minority of cases. Here, a new arrival with a history of offences against children joined vulnerable, often single parent families.

Outside perpetrators (13%), individuals sometimes unknown to the family, were involved in a small proportion of cases.

Such situations caused great concern and consumed much human energy and resources, but they were found to be rare and little about the perpetrators' behaviour was different from that already known from previous research.

If organised abuse is rare, then ritual or satanic abuse seems to be practically non-existent. La Fontaine found that the terms were misleading. While elements of ritual were identified in a handful of cases of abuse, satanic elements were never proven. Occasionally paedophiles claimed magical powers in order to control and silence children but even here allegations about devil-worship, witchcraft or animal sacrifice were invariably unfounded. Generally speaking, cases turned out to be incidents of severe abuse involving sexual, physical and emotional maltreatment. The long-term effects were those associated with sexual abuse, emotional neglect and severe material and educational deprivation.

Causes of abuse

None of the studies was designed to discover the causes of abuse although some touched on factors associated with severe or enduring punishment and with emotional neglect. Many teams commented on the quality of parents' marriages; their mental health; possible drug misuse; parents' own experiences of abuse; their age, education and religion at the time the children were born and their living conditions. However, this evidence has little to say about the causes of abuse because scrutiny falls almost exclusively upon those children who come to the notice of child protection agencies. They tend to be working class and poor; little is known about middle class parents who mistreat their offspring or about children abused outside the home.

Browne and Saqi's account of the various theories put forward since the Second World War, illustrates the relationship between definitions and perceived causes of abuse. They identify five different models which explain why children are maltreated. Among them are:

> *Psychopathic*: Fifty years ago child abuse was thought to be a rare event and North American researchers emphasised organic illness suffered by known perpetrators.
> *Social or environmental*: As abuse came to be recognised as more widespread, it was clear that not all abusers had psychiatric difficulties. Problems of housing, unemployment and other social stressors came to be seen as important triggers of abusive behaviour.
> *Special victim*: A handful of studies have emphasised the special problems facing some parents, such as those bringing up children with learning difficulties or disabilities.
> *Psycho-social*: More recent research has demonstrated how certain social and psychological factors interact to predispose some people to violent behaviour.
> *Integrated model:* Today, it is broadly accepted that a combination of social, psychological, economic and environmental factors play a part in the

abuse or neglect of children. The integrated model is broadly in line with the perspectives on abuse described in this Overview. Families overwhelmed and depressed by social problems form the greatest proportion of those assessed and supported by child protection agencies. Not included in this group is a small proportion with very different characteristics, such as those in which a parent has serious psychiatric problems or a predisposition to family violence.

How much abuse?

Even a glance at the preceding pages would suggest that estimated rates of abuse must be treated with caution. The age of the children surveyed, the way in which abuse is defined, the reliability of the information gathered (for example whether respondents have exaggerated or concealed their experiences) will determine the amount of abuse uncovered. Unwisely, prevalence rates are sometimes read as if they are comparable with one another. They are seldom so and, as a result, comparisons are frequently unreliable. It is not surprising, therefore, to find variation in the rates for sexual abuse. Finkelhor, in the United States, reported rates of six to 62% in females and three to 31% in males. Apply these data to the general population in the United Kingdom and the number of women who have been sexually abused may be anything between 300,000 and several million.

Nevertheless, it is possible to draw some conclusions about the number of children who might need help. Most children - even most toddlers in fact - are occasionally hit by their parents. If the idea of continuum is applied, hitting is to be distinguished from a severe beating. The researchers at the Thomas Coram Unit found that 16% of children had received a beating, usually on the leg or the bottom. One in ten children were hit on the head and one in twenty were kicked by their mothers. Smith's team assessed the severity of physical control, taking into account the intention or potential to cause harm and the use of implements. Most children received mild punishment but 14% had experiences which could be categorised as severe. It was rare for parents to bite or punch their children or force them to eat.

Kelly, Regan and Burton at the University of North London undertook an exploratory study of sexual abuse in a sample of 1,244 16-21 year olds at school or college. They wanted to estimate the number who had unwanted sexual experiences. Using previous studies they devised nine definitions of sexual abuse, each of increasing severity.

When they applied the least restrictive definition, they found very widespread maltreatment. Nearly three-fifths of the women and over a quarter of the men had experienced minor but nonetheless unwanted sexual attention. Some of the respondents in this category did not regard their experiences as abusive. When the definition was adjusted so that it only included behaviour which involved some physical contact between perpetrator and victim, the prevalence rates fell considerably. By the most restrictive definition, four per cent of young women and two per cent of young men had been sexually abused.

The evidence just reviewed relates to types of abuse, but is it possible to estimate the proportion of children living in low warmth, high criticism environments described earlier? This definition encompasses several forms of maltreatment and suggests that a range of services may be needed to support such children. Is it possible to put a figure on the number of children *each year* who live in such households? By any strict scientific criteria the answer must be no. But we can use the combined wisdom of the studies reviewed in this volume to make a reasonable estimate. Smith and colleagues found that three per cent of children each year find themselves in families which, for the child, are relatively cold and critical. Some physical abuse and neglect may be a feature of their upbringing and some will experience sexual abuse. Left unsupported, these children will almost certainly suffer some long-term harm and the concern of child protection agencies would certainly be warranted, although questions about maltreatment might be better subsumed in a more general scrutiny of a child's needs.

Another way of looking at this evidence is to consider the legal framework within which professionals may intervene to support or protect vulnerable children. All children living in the low warmth, high criticism environments described earlier are children in need as defined in Part III of the *Children Act*, 1989 and most of them may receive support through the routine work of professionals, particularly the preventative service of health visitors and social workers. As many as 160,000 children each year will be subject to enquiries under Section 47 of the *Children Act*, 1989 which enables the local authority to decide whether they should take any action to safeguard or promote the child's welfare. In these circumstances, child protection professionals have several options from which to choose:

THE CHILDREN ACT, 1989 defines 'children in need' in this way:
For the purposes of this Part (of the Act) a child shall be taken to be in need if,
a) he is unlikely to achieve or maintain, or to have the opportunity of achieving or maintaining, a reasonable standard of health or development without the provision for him of services by a local authority under this Part;
b) his health or development is likely to be significantly impaired, or further impaired, without the provision for him of such services; or
c) he is disabled.
'Development' means physical, intellectual, emotional, social or behavioural development; 'health' means physical or mental health.
From Sections 17(10) and (11) of the *Children Act*, 1989.

- they may decide that the health and development of the children will be significantly impaired and provide *family support* under Section 17 of the *Children Act*, 1989. Such services extend to respite care and accommodation for children who wish to live away from home
- they may decide that the child is likely to suffer significant harm and seek to make use of *child welfare services* for children looked after away from home. Where parents are unco-operative or the maltreatment is so severe as to be beyond negotiation, professionals may seek to invoke emergency powers under Part V of the 1989 Act, for example, a child assessment order or emergency protection order.

This link between Part III of the *Children Act*, 1989 and those sections concerned with enquiries and emergency proceedings for children at risk of maltreatment is frequently under-emphasised by professionals. Gibbons and colleagues, in their study of the operation of child protection registers, expressed concern about the high percentage (over 50%) of cases in which there were grounds for concern about the care children received and yet no services were provided beyond the Section 47 enquiry. The implications of this finding are discussed in the next section on the child protection process.

The problems of definition: Summary points

- Child abuse is difficult to define but clear parameters for intervention are necessary if professionals are to act with confidence to protect vulnerable children.

- Thresholds which legitimise action on the part of child protection agencies appear as the most important components of any definition of child abuse.

- The research evidence suggests that authoritative knowledge about what is known to be bad for children should play a greater part in drawing these thresholds.

- A large number of children in need live in contexts in which their health and development are neglected. For these children it is the corrosiveness of long-term emotional, physical and occasionally sexual maltreatment that causes psychological impairment or even significant harm.

- Instances of child sexual abuse may not conform to general findings about child protection. For example, minor single incidents can damage children and thresholds and criminal statutes tend to be clearer than is found when dealing with physical abuse.

The child protection process

The preceding discussion focused on definitions and prevalence of abuse. But not all children who are emotionally neglected are known to child protection agencies and the work of these organisations is not solely concerned with maltreatment. Many studies in this package of research have been concerned with the child protection process; with describing and understanding the way it works, identifying when and how to intervene, and finding out what happens when children and families are no longer under the investigative gaze. This section reviews the evidence from these studies.

It is helpful to view the children and families caught up in the child protection process in the context of all vulnerable children. Although the evidence is not absolutely conclusive, it has been estimated by Smith and colleagues that, each year, 350,000 children will be in an environment of low warmth and high criticism. These children are 'in need' to the extent that their health and development will be significantly impaired if their families do not receive some help. Many of these children will be supported through the routine work of health visitors and other preventative strategies. We do not know how many, but a proportion of these children will receive help via Section 17 of the *Children Act*, 1989 including some who are accommodated under voluntary arrangements.

Many, however, will be subject to Section 47 enquiries to establish whether the local authority needs to take action to safeguard the child, what many currently think of as the start of the child protection process. We can interpret the work of Gibbons and colleagues to suggest that about 160,000 such enquiries take place in England each year, including 25,000 where suspicions of maltreatment or neglect are unsubstantiated.

Because the decision to investigate abuse is influenced by social and administrative factors, the family characteristics of the 160,000 children dealt with under child protection procedures are not typical of families and children generally; nor are they typical of all families in which children are maltreated. Gibbons and colleagues found that over a third (36%) were headed by a lone parent and in only 30% of cases were both natural parents resident. Nearly three-fifths (57%) lacked a wage earner and over half (54%) were dependent on income support. Domestic violence (27%) and mental illness (13%) within the family also featured prominently and, in Thoburn and colleagues' study, nearly a quarter (23%) had suffered an accident or serious ill health during the previous year. One in seven parents under suspicion were known to have been abused themselves as children. Most (65%) children had previously been known to social services and a previous investigation had been undertaken in almost half (45%) of the 1,888 cases Gibbons and colleagues scrutinised. So, it is the most vulnerable in our society who are most likely to become the object of a Section 47 enquiry. What should they expect from the child protection process?

The *Children Act,* 1989 makes no mention of child protection registers or even child protection conferences. Part V of the legislation dealing with emergency proceedings, police protection and child assessment orders can be relevant, but all cases referred to the child protection process are governed by procedures described in *Working Together*. These arrangements have evolved since the 1960s. They have frequently been the subject of close public scrutiny, such as after the tragic death of Maria Colwell in 1974 and during the Cleveland Inquiry of 1987. Guidance largely concerns the ways in which agencies should co-operate to protect children from harm. It encapsulates the child protection register, a case management tool to identify those children thought to be at risk of abuse. While this provides an operational record of children requiring an inter-agency plan for their protection, the register does not indicate the proportion of children suffering maltreatment.

The diagram on page 28 describes the child protection process, showing – as accurately as the research evidence will allow – what happens each year to the 11 million children in England; it focuses especially on those dealt with under child protection procedures. The diagram also brings to notice approximately 25,000 children who come to the attention of child protection agencies even though they are found not to have been maltreated. It can be seen, first of all, that the process has four clearly identifiable stages, *pre-investigation, first enquiry, family visit,* and *conference and registration*.

HOW EFFECTIVE IS inter-agency co-operation in child protection?

It is not helpful to think of agencies being co-operative or unco-operative. Gough and colleagues propose a continuum of co-ordination between professionals, with 'working separately' at one end and 'being part of a true team' at the other.

Hallett and Birchall found that child protection co-ordination was in an intermediate position in which the anxiety of professionals ensured that they did not approach the task without the support of colleagues from other disciplines but not to the extent of fully co-ordinating roles and responsibilities. The University of Stirling team concluded that inter-agency co-operation in child protection was more to do with the exchange of information, some joint planning and the organisation of tasks than with the hands-on collaboration of professionals working together.

While relatively good inter-agency work characterised early enquiries, once protection plans had been made it tended to decline; social services were frequently left with sole responsibility.

First enquiry

Having described the characteristics of families subject to an abuse enquiry, what is it that triggers the interest of professionals? Cleaver and Freeman found that abuse came to official attention in one of three ways. Most commonly, someone, usually the child or another member of the family, disclosed their concerns to a professional; just over half (51%) of enquiries began in this way. In about two-fifths (39%) of cases, professionals already working with the family identified child abuse. In the remaining 10% of all enquiries, abuse was suggested during an unrelated event, such as an arrest or home visit.

Frequently, the first enquiry was undertaken without the knowledge of parents. The records of the agencies dealing with the enquiry were checked, colleagues in other agencies were telephoned and, if there was cause for concern, the child protection register was scanned. Gibbons and colleagues found that the register was extensively used – over 60,000 enquiries every year – more than 150 a day. Four-fifths of child protection professionals surveyed by this research team viewed the register as an essential part of the child protection process, even though for two out of three of the 160,000 initial referrals the register was not consulted.

The first stages of an abuse enquiry require that professionals work together. Hallett and Birchall found that agencies were glad to share information and spread the pressures created by suspected abuse. However, they discovered that co-operation was more likely at the beginning of the process than at the end and

IS THE CHILD protection system being used as a passport to services?

The researchers found that some children were subject to Section 47 enquiries - too often characterised as investigations - because professionals believed that this increased their chances of getting resources for services. Such practice reflects an imbalance between child protection and family support services. If local authorities act in the spirit of the *Children Act,* 1989 they will prioritise children in need and match them to appropriate services; better outcomes may then be achieved.

that professionals sought corroboration through informal checks, many of which were not recorded. As time passed, collaboration declined, so that in two-fifths of child protection plans looked at by the University of Stirling team, no other departments besides social services were mentioned. Many professionals gather to decide the best course of action but it is social workers who usually put plans into effect.

Co-operation in the later stages of the protection process depends upon a clarity of professional roles and responsibilities. Social workers and health visitors who use similar techniques of intervention often complement each other well, particularly when health visitors continue to offer support for families in need after child protection concerns have abated and, therefore, social work interest in the case has subsided. The relationship between police and social services is less easy, reflecting the sometimes conflicting aims and objectives of justice and welfare. The police, quite naturally, want to prosecute more offenders and feel frustration at not being able to gather firm evidence. Hallett and Birchall concluded that the criminal justice system's contribution to child protection was limited.

The role of teachers is particularly confused. They spend more time with children than any other professional group and education services refer the most cases to the child protection process. Nevertheless, other professionals remain unclear about the role of education in child protection and teachers remain unclear about their own contribution. Hallett and Birchall were among several researchers who emphasised the need to raise awareness in schools about the protection process.

Family visit

Over a decade ago, Dingwall stated that the most important step in a child abuse investigation occurs when an allegation becomes public property. This finding remains true. When the allegation becomes public, family members usually learn that they are under suspicion. Whatever else happens in the days, weeks, months and years following, the impact at this moment of realisation can be devastating. The Dartington and Oxford teams talked at length to parents in these early stages. The following quotation, from a mother who learned from a social worker that her son's teacher suspected sexual abuse, was typical:

> When I got the letter I was very shocked. I said 'Ah-ah .. what's happening with the social worker! What have I done? Are they coming to take my child away?' I was scared. I hoped what happened to the Orkneys isn't going to happen to me now. I was just – 'Oh, God, if anyone rings this bell, I hope – Oh God, it's not them!' Anyone who rings the bell, I look out of the window first – don't open the door – and I say 'Who is this?' From what I've heard from the telly, you know, I was very, very scared. And I phoned the social worker up. She wasn't in there! And I left a message. But I didn't get a reply from her.

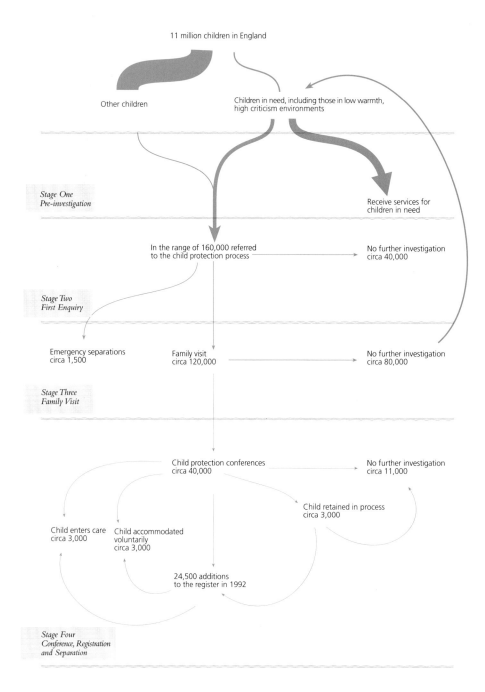

11 million children in England

Other children

Children in need, including those in low warmth,
high criticism environments

Stage One
Pre-investigation

Receive services for
children in need

In the range of 160,000 referred
to the child protection process

No further investigation
circa 40,000

Stage Two
First Enquiry

Emergency separations
circa 1,500

Family visit
circa 120,000

No further investigation
circa 80,000

Stage Three
Family Visit

Child protection conferences
circa 40,000

No further investigation
circa 11,000

Child retained in process
circa 3,000

Child enters care
circa 3,000

Child accommodated
voluntarily
circa 3,000

24,500 additions
to the register in 1992

Stage Four
Conference, Registration
and Separation

The figures are estimates using findings from the research studies extrapolated to give a picture for England. Estimates are based on the 24,500 children whose names were added to the child protection register in 1992. Whenever possible, checks with government statistics and other research have been undertaken. However, the results are not precise. Many factors, not least the fact that some children enter the process several times in one year, could not be taken into account.

As the diagram on the facing page shows, a tiny minority of parents lose their children at the point of the first enquiry, but it is this wrench, more than anything else, that parents fear. Unease which lingers as the case conference approaches hinders parental participation.

Conference and registration

Only a quarter of referrals lead to a meeting of professionals. Several weeks can elapse between the first enquiry and the meeting: Gibbons and colleagues found the interval was 34 days on average, longer than the eight days recommended in guidance. The primary function of such conferences is to assess risk and decide how best to protect the child, but Farmer and Owen discovered several others: the conference acted as a gateway to resources; it ensured that vulnerable children were subject to regular monitoring and review; more important, it provided a context in which sensitive information could be shared. Although only one conference is shown in the preceding diagram, several meetings may occur.

What do people discuss? A glance at the minutes of the last conference attended is likely to reveal that meetings are predominantly concerned with the details of an abuse incident. There will certainly be discussion of the child's health and development, the parents' past history, and the relationships within the family, especially the quality of parenting including what has worked in the past. As the previous sections illustrate, a parent's inability to cope is frequently linked to other difficulties so that conference discussions extend to housing, social support and finances.

The conference must assess risk, decide whether the child's name should be placed on the register and devise a protection plan. The plan may be passed on to other professionals to implement. The Bristol University team found that assessing risk and agonising over registration elbowed aside plans for action so that deciding what to do by way of the child protection plan was frequently pushed to the end of the meeting and lasted, on average, no more than nine minutes. As family circumstances often changed rapidly after the conference, the protection plan could quickly become out of date. It did not help if social workers found themselves implementing a plan with which they did not agree.

Working Together states that parents and sometimes older children should have a seat at this table. It is now generally agreed that levels of parent participation at conferences are an indicator of good practice. Thoburn and colleagues began their research before the revised guidelines had been implemented in 1991. They worked from the premise that families should be involved in the child protection process and chose to work in seven local authorities which were trying hard to do this. Yet even in these, nearly a third of parents either did not attend or were not invited to the conference. Recent evidence would suggest that levels of parental participation in the child protection process have improved.

GIBBONS AND COLLEAGUES looked at identification from a different angle: the source of referrals to the child protection process. Health professionals and families - those closest to the child - were the main initiators; social services, police and probation who handled the most difficult cases came lower down this list:

Sources of referral	%
Teachers, school nurses and education welfare	23
Health visitors, GPs and hospital staff	17
Household members and other lay people	17
Social services professionals	13
Police or probation	12
Anonymous	6
Other	12

Paediatric junior doctor
General practitioner
Class teacher
Consultant paediatrician
Area manager
Child protection co-ordinator
NSPCC
Solicitor/court
Education welfare
Nurse manager
Headteacher/deputy
Minute taker
Principal/team leader
Health visitor/school nurse
Police
Social worker

%

60

40

20

WHO SITS ROUND the table at a Child Protection Conference?

Hallett and Birchall looked at the attendance of 48 initial child protection conferences in two local authorities. They found that an average of 10 professionals went to these meetings and that, occasionally, as many as 16 sat around the table. The size of the conference is significant; Farmer and Owen found that the greater the number of people attending the conference, the greater were the chances of registration and clearly large gatherings are going to be intimidating to parents. This diagram indicates which professionals are most likely to be seen at an initial child protection conference.

With so many people from such a variety of backgrounds involved in each case, consensus is surprisingly high; indeed, some commentators, such as Dingwall and colleagues have suggested that the infrequency of dissent is a cause for concern. Hallett and Birchall say that levels of agreement can be explained by the relative stability of local professional networks, the context of anxiety created by the suspicion of child abuse and by the propensity of any system to limit fundamental questions about its aims and objectives.

Thoburn and colleagues constructed a scale of parental involvement which placed partnership with parents at the top and no involvement, manipulation or placation at the bottom. In the first six months of a child protection case, full partnership was achieved for only three per cent of the 378 family members surveyed. Given the pain that parents experience at the outset of an abuse investigation and the very real differences in parents' and professionals' objectives, perhaps it was unrealistic to expect much more. A degree of involvement and consultation was partially achieved but could have occurred with greater frequency and consistency. Parents viewed the help being offered more sympathetically if they were fully involved in the decision making process, a situation that also eased the professional task. Getting parents to participate is skilful work but has long-term benefits in that it is shown to be associated with greater success in achieving subsequent family participation.

Whether or not parents are there, the conference has to decide what to do next. One of the principal, although not the only, course of action is to place the child's name on the register. The four main categories of registration suggested in *Working Together*, namely neglect, physical injury, sexual abuse and emotional

THOBURN'S FINDINGS on parents' attendance at case conferences:	
Parents attend	%
All conference	21
Part of conference	40
End of conference	8
Don't attend	19
Are not invited	13

IS THE CHILD PROTECTION register used appropriately?
The placing of a child's name on the protection register is meant to provide a focal point to which agencies can speedily refer when concerned about possible harm to the child. This is clear in *Working Together*, paragraph 6.37. Although professionals value the register, it is not consulted for 60% of the children about whom there is professional concern. Despite clear guidance, registration has assumed several other functions. It protects professionals from the consequences of practice shortcomings, it obtains scarce resources and facilitates the construction of an inter-agency protection plan for the child. The researchers found confusion between assessing risk and planning, intervention and registration, all of which should have clear and specific functions.

abuse, are still those most frequently used. There is a dislike of mixed categories, although Gibbons and colleagues found that two-fifths of custodians also used the labels 'non-organic failure to thrive' or 'child in the same household as a person previously involved in abuse'.

It is well known that there is considerable geographical variation in the rate at which children in England and Wales have their names placed on the child protection register. In Gloucestershire, for example, the rate on the 31st of March 1992 was 0.8 per 1,000, compared with 5.4 in East Sussex. The rate is 10.0 per 1,000 in Southwark but only 4.4 in Tower Hamlets. It is probable that levels of registration only partially reflect levels of abuse, so these considerable variations must be caused by other factors. Little and Gibbons identified two sets of factors which explained much of the difference. The first were socio-demographic factors, such as levels of poverty and services to help those in need. Second, there were factors associated with the way the register was operated.

If the following indicators apply in a local authority, it is likely that the child protection register rate will be relatively high. Addressing these issues - particularly those associated with the operational factors - should give ACPCs the means to reduce the rate of children on the register; but changing the rate will not necessarily improve the situation of abused children or the service they are offered.

Socio-demographic factors	Operational factors
High rate of children in care	Family support services in short supply
High rate of births to unmarried mothers	Dead children included on register
High unemployment rate	Specific criteria for removing children's names
Poor playgroup provision	Child protection plans not automatically linked
Plentiful day nursery provision	to registration
High rate of residents in council	No regular updating of register
accommodation	Decentralised organisation
Low numbers of social workers per resident	No local specialised child protection posts

The register has come to be seen by professionals as an essential tool. They see it as giving case conferences a focus and fostering inter-agency co-operation. In short, it has become a pivotal part of the planning of child protection services, including training and supervision. Nonetheless, in the later stages of intervention it is frequently social services who are left holding the case.

Thresholds for action

The protection process just described seems to have some strengths. It deals with a considerable volume of work, up to 160,000 cases annually. Just over 15% of these children have to be formally registered and in 96 out of every 100 cases the children remain at home with relatives. Moreover, whatever the deficiencies of the process, it will be seen that most children are protected from abuse.

Gibbons and colleagues expressed concern that so many cases were drawn into the process. They compared it to trawling for fish, casting,

> a small meshed net in which a large number of minnows – which have later to be discarded – are caught as well as the marketable fish. Each fleet has its own mesh…

to which could be added,

> …and several net designs are being used.

Protection issues are best viewed in the context of children's wider needs. It is important to ensure that inappropriate cases do not get caught up in the child protection process, for this could have several undesirable consequences. Of particular concern is the unnecessary distress caused to family members who may then be unwilling to co-operate with subsequent plans. Professionals have to weigh up which stages in the protection process are relevant to each case. They may have to rebuild a sense of trust with family members to enable them to participate. Ultimately, it will be necessary to decide when and how to permit a case to leave the child protection arena. It is to these issues that we turn next.

The *Children Act, 1989* requires local authorities to provide a range of services for children in need and intends that only extreme cases will require adjudication by courts. For all but the most serious cases there are many intermediate stages between a child first coming to the notice of welfare agencies, the removal of the child from home and/or a court hearing being necessary. The child protection process encompasses some of these stages. The idea of a 'threshold' which includes the criteria for moving a child from one stage in the process to another has been introduced. In the following pages several thresholds for action are described, as are the criteria on which they are based.

Working Together clearly states the threshold which must be passed before a child's name can be placed on the child protection register. Paragraph 6.39 states:

> the conference must decide that there is, or is a likelihood of, significant harm leading to the need for a child protection plan. One of the following requirements needs to be satisfied: (i) there must be one or more identifiable incidents which can be described as having adversely affected the child …Professional judgement is that further incidents are likely: or (ii) significant harm is expected on the basis of professional judgement of findings of the investigation in this individual case or on research evidence.

This is the formal test of whether concerted efforts to protect the child will be necessary. But there are other factors influencing a professional's decision to act. Important among these is some certainty that the child has been badly treated. A decade ago, Dingwall and colleagues noted that social workers used two types of evidence to identify and confirm child abuse:

- evidence on the child's clinical condition (which tended towards under-identification)
- evidence on the nature of the child's social environment (which tended towards over-identification).

As the earlier sections illustrated, in addition to this attempt to establish the facts, professionals also make moral judgements about children and families. The Bristol University team note that many conferences took into account the situation of the suspected abuser. Naturally, some form of risk assessment was a part of the conferences studied but professionals' attempts to predict the future seldom included outcome evidence. That is to say, it is rare for a conference participant to propose a particular strategy because research evidence suggests that in consequence outcomes for the child would be better.

Several research teams found that threshold decisions frequently reflected the resources available. Stepping over the threshold from first enquiry to family visit means that a child protection professional has to *do* something. This can be a disincentive to act but, after a visit, families will expect something to happen. Stepping over the next threshold from visit to case conference can be a means of obtaining resources for vulnerable families. Here, the different interests of the professions become manifest. Thoburn and colleagues found that social workers and their managers usually wanted to raise the threshold to avoid being inundated with extra work or to diminish the adverse consequences of the process on families. Other professionals, such as health visitors and teachers, often sought a lower threshold because they regarded a protection meeting as the only way to secure services. Moreover, there can be similar divisions even inside social services departments. Where agencies provide extensive Part III services, social workers tend to have a high threshold. Where staff see their role as being largely about child protection, they will lower the threshold in order to trawl every case and make it easier to offer services.

When identifying the principles on which threshold decisions are based, it is important to say what *does not* play a large part in discussions. The type of maltreatment does not feature as highly as is commonly thought, nor is severity of abuse a key indicator, although a child who has endured repeated sexual abuse is more likely to pass through each stage of the child protection process than one who suffered a single bruise. What, then, does determine a child's progress through the system?

Factors associated with progress through the child protection process

Many of the research teams that explored the issue identified factors associated with moving from one stage in the child protection process to another. Their findings can be summarised as follows:

A   It is unlikely that anything other than a first enquiry (Stage Two in the diagram on Page 28) will happen if:
there is no man in the household
it is a suspected case of neglect or emotional abuse
it is not a particularly serious accusation
the suspected perpetrator does not live with the child
the source of the referral is anonymous

A*contd*   *the case is new to social services*

there have been no previous legal orders.

B   If a family visit is undertaken, it is unlikely that a conference (Stage Four in the diagram on Page 28) will happen if:

there are only girls in the family

it is a suspected case of neglect or emotional abuse

it is not a particularly serious accusation

the suspected perpetrator does not live in the household

none of the parents has a criminal record or a history of mental illness.

C   If a conference is called, it is unlikely that the child's name will be placed on the child protection register and/or the child removed from home if:

the suspected perpetrator is not the male parent or is an outsider

the suspicion does not concern sexual abuse

police and social services are not the investigative agencies taking the lead

family members have no previous record of child abuse or criminal behaviour

the family has a single problem rather than multiple problems

the concerns are not pressed by the school.

Gibbons and colleagues devised a measure of protection to see if the children who moved from Stage Three to Stage Four of the process, that is to say from family visit to case conference, were those for whom a conference was necessary. They found that:

- for cases of physical abuse, unsubstantiated accusations were very unlikely to reach a case conference but that in some which failed to meet the threshold, children remained at risk of future maltreatment
- for cases of neglect, few reach case conferences, with the result that many highly vulnerable children failed to benefit from those resources potentially available
- for cases of sexual abuse, few conferences are held unnecessarily and few high risk cases fail to be dealt with appropriately
- thresholds differed between ACPC areas. Thus, a case could reach a case conference in one local authority but have little further action taken in another. However, differences diminished when the background characteristics of children were taken into account.

Children in need of protection

It should be clear from the preceding discussion that there is some overlap between protection work and other services provided for children in need. Many of the researchers asked the question 'would some children caught in the child protection net benefit more from family support under Section 17 of the *Children Act, 1989?*' After all, the circumstances of families dealt with under Sections 17 and

47 of the Act are frequently much the same, as are the services they ultimately receive. However, if questions of abuse are in the air, the intervention is framed differently and parents are likely to be less receptive to social workers than they would be if the approach was directed at helping a vulnerable child in need. The consequences of choosing one route or the other can be considerable. The researchers showed that resources were more likely to be allocated if the child was suspected of being abused; placing his or her name on the register was often a way of getting help for a child, although family members often disagreed with this procedure.

The perspectives on child protection adopted here indicate the advantages of looking at maltreatment in the context of children's wider needs. The way in which help is offered to families is plainly going to be important. Gibbons and colleagues felt that the emphasis on abuse was too great in many cases dealt with under a child protection banner, especially as one third of families were well known to social workers and could be approached without the spectre of child abuse being raised. Farmer and Owen found that involving the police early in investigations could be counter-productive, for instance with regard to the increased likelihood of the child being removed. Thoburn's team captured the general tenor of findings:

> the child protection process works as well as it can with the most severe cases, it works reasonably well when there is an unproved allegation of serious abuse (especially if services are sensitively offered) but it works less well with needy families who resent being brought into the 'abuse' system.

Professionals sometimes forget that the administrative routes selected for cases mean little to parents. An over-emphasis on protection issues may lead to some needs of families being overlooked and a failure to use all the services on offer. The research teams identified different types of need in the families they studied. In some cases it was a specific issue of maltreatment that caused concern but usually abuse was just one of a multitude of problems that beset the family. Others families were coping with the knowledge that someone outside the home had abused their child. Sensitivity to the different requirements and anxieties of family members, which takes account of how they will regard the help being offered, will enhance the protection provided for children.

Needless to say, much of this is easier to promise than to deliver. Each of the decisions taken by professionals will coincide with some assessment of risk to the child. Farmer and Owen found that family circumstances changed, that new abuse emerged and old concerns subsided. Child protection plans soon became outdated but conference decisions can have unexpected and lingering consequences. Far better to build a sound plan, incorporate contingencies and keep an open mind about the possibilities for change. A good plan would set out the ends to be achieved, the means to get to those ends and be mindful of the risks in this strategy, by listing things that might go wrong.

From support to treatment

Local authorities have a range of services to help and support children in need and their families. For most, this involves some direct financial assistance or, more commonly, by paying for childminders, playgroup or family centre places. The value of such support should not be underestimated – it keeps families together and forms the basis for a preventative strategy. For this to be effective, professionals must work together, but the evidence from Hallett and Birchall would suggest that while there is good inter-agency co-operation at the point of assessing risk to a child, when it comes to delivering services, there is less sharing and a poor allocation of roles; in many cases social services are left to shoulder much of the responsibility. But what social workers provide is not treatment in a clinical sense, nor does intervention involve the child leaving home for anything longer than a few hours.

The researchers consistently found that professionals confused therapy and support and, because practitioners remember the most difficult cases, they can overestimate the proportion of children separated from home. The previous evidence showed that no more than four per cent of all children coming to the notice of protection agencies and just over one-sixth of those whose names are registered leave home and it is known from research at Dartington into children looked after that 70% of victims of abuse are eventually reunited with family members, nearly always their mothers.

The problem is deciding when to move a child into treatment and then finding the appropriate service. The Family Services Study at Oxford found that even in cases of sexual abuse, the transition was haphazard. They estimated that while two-fifths of children in such circumstances received a high level of social work contact and some therapy, many needed more than the routine work of health and social work professionals, an important finding in view of Monck and New's conclusion that only a very small number of children received treatment. Moreover, follow-up studies of sexually abused children are rare and the relationship between outcome and children's needs on entering treatment is not well understood.

In cases of sexual abuse the perpetrator may be in need of treatment as well as the victim. The same may also be true for physical and emotional maltreatment but there are few, if any, clinical programmes for the abuser in such circumstances. Morgan and Barker showed that the limited service available was provided by the probation service and that information about its efficacy was in short supply. The task can be complicated when, as quite often happens, therapy offered to perpetrators brings to light the fact that they have been abused themselves as children.

By comparison, much more is known about the care careers of children looked after by social services but, even here, knowledge about the benefits of such interventions for children who have been sexually abused or grossly physically maltreated is poor. The skills needed by foster parents to look after victims of sexual abuse remain unclear and unformulated as are the particular needs of female victims, especially when they are looked after by relatives. The research programme has more to say about supporting children at home with their families than about appropriate therapy or the need for separation.

Working with and not against families

Whether professionals offer support services or therapy, remove the child or keep the family together, the benefits of involving the family in decisions about their future emerge clearly in several studies. Partnership with parents is now a feature of legislation and guidance but Thoburn and colleagues found that social workers wanted to work with families because they believed it would make their practice more effective. Wanting partnership is a step in the right direction but achieving it is difficult. A positive attitude to partnership needs to underpin action, a fact emphasised by their finding that partnership with parents tended to follow from involving the child in the process. One of the parents in the University of East Anglia study said of a social worker who claimed to be working *with* the family,

> 'she didn't care about us. All she was interested in was doing a good job, doing it by the book!'.

IN PLANNING their study, Thoburn and colleagues sought a definition of partnership in the context of child protection work. They were much influenced by the definition provided by the Family Rights Group in their publication *The Children Act, 1989: Working in Partnership with Families*. They say that partnership is marked by:
- respect for one another
- rights to information
- accountability
- competence and value accorded to any individual's contribution.

In short, each partner is seen as having something to offer, power is shared, decisions are made jointly and roles are not only respected but backed by legal and moral rights.

Some of the evidence was collected prior to the revised version of *Working Together* published in 1991 which encourages greater parental involvement, particularly in conferences, so it is likely that patterns of partnership will have changed. As will be seen later, partnership usually leads to better outcomes for children. Thoburn's team found that meaningful participation was apparent in only a fifth of cases where the child's name had been placed on the register and in only 12% of cases at the investigation stage. This suggests that much remains to be done in engineering parental participation. More encouraging is the finding that parents were seldom totally excluded from the process or manipulated by professionals.

Farmer and Owen concluded that an understanding between parents and professionals was most likely to occur if there was agreement about
- whether the child had been abused
- who was responsible
- who was to blame, and
- whether the child was at future risk.

As the following pages illustrate, disagreement – real or perceived – greatly hindered the ability of social workers to achieve desired outcomes for children. Getting things right at this stage benefited other aspects of professionals' practice. Thoburn and colleagues found that greater parental involvement in the successive stages of a child protection investigation led to
- more purposeful social work
- more creative ways of undertaking family assessments after protection conferences, particularly when managers supported such a strategy.

Withdrawing support

The evidence reviewed so far demonstrates the strengths and weaknesses of the child protection process. One important deficiency concerns the way in which families leave the system. In common with many other social systems, while professionals jealously guard the point of entry, less attention is given to the point of exit. Whether it is the practitioner seeking to limit caseloads, the perspectives of anxious parents worrying that they might lose their children or the dispassionate gaze of the scientist measuring outcomes – whatever the perspective, leaving this system is seldom tidy.

To an extent some lingering ambiguity is to be expected. It is hard to gather evidence that is absolutely conclusive. Thus, it is not surprising that Gibbons and colleagues found that half the abuse allegations were not substantiated; they were neither proven nor disproved. Consequently, professionals struggle to communicate confidence and certainty to the family. It is difficult under these circumstances to remove with equanimity the child's name from the register. Better to be on the safe side. While erring on the side of caution and leaving the child 'registered' may cause distress to parents, professionals risk media criticism and even legal challenge should precipitate de-registration be followed by serious re-abuse. Despite offering partnership to parents, the protection process incorporates functions which families are unlikely to accept. Unfortunately, proffered partnership cannot conceal from parents less welcome aspects of child protection procedures. The register, which is intended to alert professionals to the fact that a child is at risk, will often be regarded by parents as a punitive measure or as a constraint to ensure their compliance.

Sharland and colleagues found that parents in cases of child sexual abuse were often left in limbo - they did not know if they had been found guilty or innocent, in need of help or self-sufficient, safe with their children or still under the watchful eye of child protection officials. Gibbons and colleagues remarked that de-registration (one of several exit points from the child protection process) had few general rules and usually occurred when the original concerns evaporated. Child-care studies charting children's progress over time have shown that the conclusion of one part of the care process does not always signal the end of inter-agency planning; it frequently marks the start of another phase.

To many parents, the idea of 'opening' and 'closing' a case has the flavour of the police station and court rather than of the surgery or clinic. Removal of their child's name from the register returns parents, somewhat tarnished, to the ranks of the orthodox. This is in strong contrast to professional perspectives where 'case' frequently confers visions of medical consultants, continuities of care and benign confirming oversight.

Professionals are taught to tolerate a degree of confusion, to manage probability and possibility and to keep emotional distance. Parents are not. The professional knows that a decision to leave a child's name off the register is not the equivalent of taking no further action, although it can amount to something similar in practice if registration is seen as the only means of obtaining resources. Similarly, taking a name off the register does not mean withdrawing help; indeed the Bristol University team found that one in ten de-registrations occurred because the original registration was counter-productive and help could be better offered without it. Quite clearly de-registration was not an end in itself. Parents, on the other hand, find lack of clarity on the part of the state's agencies difficult to understand. Their own lives may be chaotic but statutory agencies appear to parents to represent order and predictability. Monck and New noted in cases of child sexual abuse some parents wanted clear guidance on what they could do to protect their children and manage disturbed behaviour.

The Dartington team, concerned with the broad spectrum of cases, put it more strongly. Parents wanted to know when an investigation was open and closed. Given the trauma caused by the original suspicion, they deserved a letter explaining how the matter had been resolved. Many families bruised by investigation need encouragement to, once more, welcome social services should the need arise. Above all else, parents need clarity - both at the beginning (to know that their child is highly unlikely to be taken away) and at the end (to know the accusation is proven, disproved or still in doubt).

The child protection process: Summary points

- Many children who have experienced low warmth, high criticism environments come to the notice of social, health and other welfare services. Some 160,000 are subject to Section 47 enquiries each year, including a small proportion for whom concerns are probably ill-founded.

- Families caught in the child protection process are, in the main, multiply disadvantaged, a characteristic not always found in the wider population of abused children. Nearly all (96%) of these children remain at home and the majority of those separated are swiftly reunited.

- Child protection enquiries seek not only to establish whether maltreatment has occurred but also to gauge whether the family can benefit from support services. Too frequently, enquiries become investigations and, in over half of cases, families receive no services as the result of professionals' interest in their lives.

- There are several thresholds dividing the different parts of the child protection process. Many enquiries take place without parents' knowledge and the decision to make a family visit, and the handling of this visit, have ramifications for later parts of the process. Decisions about registration or removal tend to receive undue salience and could be better balanced against plans to support the child and family in the months after the case conference. As is often the case in social systems, professionals are far less concerned with the way families are left when the enquiry is complete and concerns subside than they are with the way children enter the protection process.

- As nearly all of the children remain at or return home, involving the family in the child protection process is likely to be effective. The research adds weight to this argument but finds that professionals could be doing more to achieve a partnership with both parents and, where appropriate, the child.

How effective is the child protection process?

Of the 20 studies reviewed here, ten followed up children to see whether their situation had improved. The difficulty of studying and evaluating outcomes (which are one of the four influences on the thresholds for action described earlier) is discussed by Roy Parker and colleagues in *Looking After Children:Assessing Outcomes in Child Care*. As with so much else, the concept of outcome is far from simple.

They explain that outcomes cannot be regarded as free-standing states waiting to be discovered and evaluated; they are products of complex processes of selection, shaped by the interplay of different interests, assumptions and aspirations. Hence people dealing with similar circumstances will value different things. For example, the clinical interests of a therapist monitoring a child's progress are not necessarily those of an accountant seeking value for money. The criteria used to evaluate outcomes also change over time: 30 years ago divorce and unemployment were acceptable indicators of adult malaise in a way that would be unlikely today.

How is the child protection process to be judged? A key test of outcome must be whether children are protected from abuse and whether they function and develop satisfactorily. This is the logical conclusion of the welfare principle, the measure of which must take into consideration a child's family relations, health and educational experiences and assess his or her attainments, wishes, adaptations and happiness.

But, other criteria are possible. As nearly all children who have been abused continue to live with their families, even after they have been temporarily moved to foster homes or residential care, the gains and losses for other family members need also to be considered. One must remember, too, that services which protect children are publicly organised and financed and are legally directed, which suggests other important outcomes, not least the extent to which scandalous events are prevented, children's and families' rights are respected, money is well spent and standards are maintained. Finally, since child-care is a professional service, cases need to be judged according to the progress children make in response to our efforts and the manner in which any change comes about.

Each research study set its own parameters and considered particular outcomes for particular people, which were measured in particular ways. These peculiarities need to be borne in mind when considering the evidence. Apart from the cases in Gibbons and colleagues' work on child protection registers, most children were well into the protection system by the time they were first followed up. Three sets of outcomes for abused children are important and each is explained in turn:

- the effects of abuse on children
- the extent to which children are protected
- the effects of abuse enquiries on families.

The effects of abuse on children

Only the study by Gibbons, Gallagher and colleagues sought to elaborate on the effects of child abuse. There is already an extensive literature on this issue which is discussed by the authors of the published studies. Further authoritative sources are listed in the reference section at the back of this book, for instance, articles by Skuse and Bentovim on physical abuse, Smith and Bentovim on sexual abuse and Hobbs and colleagues on neglect, failure to thrive and other adverse conditions. Even so, to understand the risks that need to be addressed, it is helpful to reiterate the possible consequences of abuse.

Links between childhood experiences and adult adjustments are debatable, but it is generally agreed that abuse is a serious risk factor. Abused children appear more likely to suffer intellectually and as social beings and to display affective and behaviour disorders by comparison with non-abused children from similar backgrounds. Nevertheless, long-term harm is not an automatic consequence of abuse, neither is damage irreparable. This much has been demonstrated in research in which the impact of the abuse itself has been disentangled from the contributing circumstances and the results of intervention.

These varied effects can be seen in the long-term experience of physically abused children described in the work of Gibbons, Gallagher and colleagues. Their follow-up study of children registered in the early 1980s and the comparison with a group of non-abused children from similar backgrounds uncovered a complex picture. Those in the abused group were more likely to show behaviour problems at home and school, had greater difficulty with friendships, scored lower on certain cognitive tests and, more commonly, lived at the follow-up stage in families headed by a lone parent; but in individual cases it was difficult to ascribe a child's circumstances or state of health to any aspect of their lives at the time they were maltreated. Thus, isolated incidents of physical abuse in the context of a non-violent family and in the absence of sexual abuse or neglect did not necessarily lead to poor long-term outcomes for children. As significantly, outcomes tended to be worse for both groups whenever neglect came into the picture, reinforcing the significance of the high risk context discussed earlier.

Were the children protected?

Research conducted in the 1960s and 70s found alarmingly high rates for the physical re-abuse of children. Some 60% or more suffered in this way. However, these figures are now viewed with caution as they reflect the severity of cases in the study samples. In an assessment of evidence from numerous recent studies, Gibbons, Gallagher and colleagues argue that lower abuse rates are a more accurate reflection of the risk currently faced by children entering the child protection arena.

The research in this programme supports this conclusion by showing that between a quarter and a third of children were known to have been re-abused after they came to the notice of the child protection agencies. Looking at cases

HOW EFFECTIVE IS the child protection process in dealing with heavy end referrals? None of the researchers concluded that heavy end cases were being missed or ignored by the system, although this can happen. Their main concern was that interventions were often limited in scope because of their restrictive emphasis on abuse. Non-abusing parents' requests for psychiatric help were overlooked, non-resident parents were rarely engaged, the needs of siblings were ignored and children were placed in foster and residential homes where further maltreatment occurred. Greatest criticism was reserved for the experiences of families for whom there is less concern. Too many minor cases were rigorously investigated with the result that a large number of minnows, which later had to be discarded, got caught up in the protection net. This can have bad effects. Parents become alienated and, even when abuse suspicions are not substantiated, can face distress and hardship, both of which make life difficult for the children whom agencies seek to help.

A more effective approach in many situations where abuse is relatively minor is to tackle the causes of maltreatment by means of enquiry followed by family assessment, followed by, where appropriate, support services, rather than with heavy handed investigations which leave the family unassisted. This is viable given that half of the families involved in the protection process have multiple problems and are already well known to welfare agencies.

entering the system early, Cleaver and Freeman found that after families were confronted with suspicion, 26% of children were thought to have been re-abused in the following two years. These figures are echoed by Farmer and Owen who found that, in the 20 months following registration for abuse of all kinds, 25% had been subsequently abused and a further 5% had 'been left without safeguards'. Similarly, Thoburn and colleagues found that 'one in five children were actually or suspected of being re-abused' in the following six months. Of those registered for physical abuse, Gibbons, Gallagher and colleagues found that ten years on, 20% were known to have been re-abused physically and 5% sexually. Most of this maltreatment occurred within two years of registration. For sexual abuse, the Oxford study defined 43% of the cases investigated as 'unsafe' nine months later.

Some comfort can be gained from the fact that rates for serious abuse were very much lower. None of the cases in the Cleaver and Freeman study (and just 2% in Thoburn and colleagues') required medical treatment. However, those risks that did occur were varied and not necessarily a repetition of previous experience. Children who had been physically abused were sometimes abused sexually or emotionally and vice versa, or else, another child in the family could become a victim or a new perpetrator could emerge.

The effects of abuse investigations on families

The Cleveland Report emphasised the traumatic effects that an abuse investigation can have on families. All the studies confirm the sense of shock, fear and anger felt at the point of confrontation and the lingering bitter aftertaste. On the brighter side, there is evidence that although some trauma may remain, relations between social workers and parents often improve. Both the Dartington and Bristol studies found that in 70% of cases, parents became more sympathetic to professional concern and came to regard the enquiry as having been in some way beneficial. The resultant social work was shown to promote better health, living conditions and parenting skills and to enhance a child's physical and mental development.

Other consequences were not as favourable. Suspicion and accusation could also be followed by worsening family relationships, leading to recrimination, marital breakdown, economic hardship and sometimes homelessness; all severe setbacks to a child's quality of life. Nine of the 23 two-parent families in Cleaver and Freeman's study broke up within two years of the accusation and only two of the mothers concerned subsequently formed new relationships. While these figures may not be all that different from those for the general population, and in some situations separation may have been beneficial, they echo Farmer and

Owen's conclusion that the needs of the main carer or parent were met in only 30% of their cases. This has serious implications, since failure to meet the needs of parents will inevitably have an impact on the happiness of children. Except in very extreme cases, the needs of parents and children cannot be compartmentalised.

How effective is the child protection process? Summary points

- The measurement of outcomes is difficult but necessary to assess how far the aims of child protection services are achieved. It also helps professionals to link cause and effect, view individual cases in the context of all vulnerable children, avoid over-generalisation and inappropriate contrasts, such as supposed conflict between the rights of children and the rights of families.

- The law on child protection seems to be appropriate and, for a majority of children, protection is secured within the family or with the family's involvement.

- The findings present a varied picture. While the child protection process has a considerable range of services directed towards children in need, these should not be deployed in a way that overwhelms clients or greatly circumscribes parental responsibility and autonomy.

- The conclusion that between a quarter and a third of the children studied were re-abused is disquieting but concern is tempered somewhat by the low incidence of severe maltreatment.

- Many studies undertook follow-ups in cases caught up in later stages of the child protection process. If the starting point had been earlier, for example with the 160,000 children subject to a Section 47 enquiry, figures for re-abuse would be lower. Nevertheless, all re-abuse is undesirable and professionals' actions can help to prevent it.

- A suspicion of child abuse has traumatic effects on families. Good professional practice can ease parents' anxiety and lead to co-operation that helps protect the child.

How can professionals best protect children?

If 'quite good but could be better' is a fair verdict on levels of re-abuse, what guidance does the research offer on how to ensure children's safety? Although they approached the issue from different angles, it is significant that all the studies identified five pre-conditions of effective practice to protect children and promote their welfare:

> sensitive and informed professional/client relationships
> an appropriate balance of power between participants
> a wide perspective on child protection
> effective supervision and training of social workers
> services which enhance children's general quality of life.

If these conditions prevail, outcomes for children are generally better at all stages of the protection process. This is a key finding of the research programme. Clearly, the characteristics of each case will modify the scope for intervention and there will be exceptions, but, demonstrably, it is the nature and quality of professional work, whether at initial referral, investigation, decision making or case closure, that generates most improvement.

Plainly, some changes that affect children will occur independently; for example, household members will come and go, economic circumstances will fluctuate and tensions subside, but professional interventions will still have a discernible effect. What qualities produce optimal outcomes for children?

Sensitive and informed professional/client relations

The most important condition for success is the quality of the relationship between a child's family and the professionals responsible. Terms used in the research publications vary: alliance, empowerment, support and information all occur, but each implies a conscious attempt to incorporate the family into the investi-gation and protection plan, including those situations where children need to be looked after away from home. At the start of an investigation, when parents may be confronted or accused, sensitivity to the first emotional reaction is key, as is the need to seek some measure of agreement about the nature and severity of the abuse. There should be an awareness also of the child's need for privacy and of the stigma associated with abuse, especially in cases of sexual abuse. An alliance is needed which involves parents and, if possible, children, actively in the investigation, which takes account of their views and incorporates their goals into plans.

Failure to achieve this level of co-operation helps to explain why some children remain safe when others do not. The quality of the relationship between parents and professionals was found to be the main reason: a recurrence of abuse was less common in those families where some agreement had been reached between professionals and family members about the legitimacy of the enquiry and the solutions adopted.

However, poor outcomes should not necessarily be taken as evidence of professional failure. Important as it is, a skilled intervention can be outweighed by the nature and severity of the case; even the best practice may be unable to alter the course of events. Thoburn and colleagues highlight a unanimous conclusion:

> The process of intervention does not appear to have an unequivocal
> impact on all cases but does seem to have a discernible effect on the
> unfolding of cases in the aftermath of referral. Perceptions on the inter-
> vention process by both parents and children were affected by the quality
> of the professional approach and this, in turn, was related to the likelihood
> that a successful partnership between parents and professionals would
> become established.

How, then, can discrepancies between clients' wishes and services offered be dealt with? One contentious issue is bridging the gap between the gender and ethnic background of professionals and clients. The studies also draw attention to the potential benefit of changing social workers at different stages of the investigation or should a serious personality clash occur. Provided such arrangements were not being manipulated by parents seeking a sympathetic ear and did not cause disruption for the child, better results often followed.

There is also agreement about the style of intervention that seems to work best with both children and families. Honesty and reliability were particularly valued. Clearly presented information about what was happening and the options available were both very important. Parents and children also wanted to be directed to sources of support, whether local groups, national associations or help-lines. Unfortunately, complaints procedures were uncommon and, where they did exist, were rarely understood or used by dissatisfied clients. In addition, the rights of participants were frequently left vague.

There were vivid examples of such shortcomings. The Family Services study at Oxford, for example, found that sexually abused children were often encouraged to speak out on the basis of a promise that the perpetrator would be 'put away'. Yet, criminal prosecution in such cases is rare and conviction is by no means certain. Failure in such delicate circumstances sometimes generated a deep sense of betrayal among children.

Farmer and Owen gave another example of how action intended to promote children's welfare produced the opposite effect:

> Children gained from being protected but felt they were not properly
> informed or consulted about what was happening, and felt a loss of
> control over what actually happened to them. After children had talked
> about the abuse they often felt responsible for the effect this had on the
> family. Indeed, they were often held responsible by family members. They
> harboured strong feelings of self-blame and often viewed the expulsion of
> the abuser with guilt and their own separation as punishment. Some
> children were also subject to gossip and bullying, and this could be
> somewhat reduced if there were tighter curbs on information which is
> released about parents when they are prosecuted.

Achieving the right balance of power between professionals, parents, other relatives and children

In a child abuse enquiry, one would not expect much power to be given to parents: the child's interests must come first and relatives might well be implicated in the maltreatment. However it emerged from the studies that as cases progressed, an inquisitorial stance was less than useful and that professionals tended to hold on to their authority long after absolute control served any purpose. Parents needed an opportunity to speak their mind and to feel that the enquiry was 'fair' even when they recognised that their influence on events was likely to be small. A great deal of social work research shows that clients will co-operate even if it is against their obvious personal interests as long as they see the process as 'just'. As one practitioner observed, 'parents need a balance that is manageable'.

All the studies highlighted the significance of the initial child protection conference in the formation of power relationships and for showing parents their true situation, but when the studies were being undertaken, too little attention was paid to the way meetings were organised. The layout of the room, the presentation of the agenda, the preparation of parents and the information given to them, the manner of introductions and the style of the language in which the proceedings are conducted all can convey stark messages to children and parents. What may be functional for getting a quick decision may confound hopes of subsequent co-operation. Delays and conflict between the priorities of professionals and parents can exacerbate difficulties and aggravate a parent's sense of confusion and alienation.

Regular exchange of information is another important feature of good professional/client relationships. Yet, the research showed that once an enquiry was complete, particularly if it was inconclusive, communications fade. Parents were rarely told when the investigation was over or what had been decided. They were left in limbo. While open-ended, low key enquiries were often a relatively inconsequential task for busy professionals, the anxiety and uncertainty they caused parents was considerable. A procedure for informing parents about the conclusion of the process would help reduce the trauma of finding themselves under suspicion.

IS PARTNERSHIP relevant to child protection?

The quality and extent of partnership between professionals and families are major factors affecting the progress of cases and outcomes for children (with the exception of some extreme cases where the abuse is very serious or the families antagonistic).
But partnership varies in quality and extent. In a quarter of cases it was not achieved despite auspicious circumstances. Agency policy and procedures or social work practice, or both together, account for much of this failure. Partnership is manifest at different stages of the process. In initial discussions with parents, the provision of information is helpful. At a protection meeting, preparation, understanding of procedures, physical layout and styles of interaction are important. In fashioning a care plan, clarity of roles and predictability are essential whereas in subsequent reviews, parents' wider needs should be addressed.

The need for a wide perspective on child protection

A third feature of good practice is the need for professionals to take a broad view of the presenting problems. This was highlighted by the Bristol University team who considered the cases of 44 children 20 months after they had been the subject of a protection meeting. It was found that while 70% of the children had been completely protected from abuse and 68% had benefited in welfare terms, in only 30% of cases had the needs of the parents or carers been met. This meant that success in all three areas was achieved for only 23%.

There were several reasons why one child in three should have fared badly in welfare terms. Placements away from home were not always satisfactory, for example, a child in a residential school became the victim of bullying. Other cases were closed or given low priority, leaving problems neglected or unrecognised. The need for treatment to help a child overcome the effects of abuse also tended to be overlooked, as were behaviour problems which required specialist help. All resulted from a failure to view child protection in a sufficiently broad context. Depression, poor self-esteem and disturbed behaviour which often pre-date an allegation are common results of abuse and are not necessarily resolved merely by guaranteeing protection.

A bias in the service towards assessment rather than prevention and treatment was noted by several researchers and their findings underline the need to tackle the wider welfare requirements of children and families. Children like services they see as being directed to their needs, but their protection is also enhanced by dealing with the health, economic and relationship problems that beset their families. Welfare and protection should be complementary.

An approach that encourages a perspective on cases as *children in need in circumstances where there may be a protection problem* is more likely to lead to a wider range of services being used to ensure the child's safety and recovery. Several researchers found that once children were registered, the attention too readily focused on the question 'what must be done to get them off?' to the detriment of 'what are their needs?' Elaborate inter-agency work was conducted during referral and enquiry but later support was often confined to contributions from a single agency. It might help if particular family problems were linked to different services and if the activity of an investigating social worker was complemented by the efforts of colleagues to offer support, advice and material help to families in trouble. At the time of the research, such arrangements were uncommon.

The main advantage of a wider look, however, is that it shifts the focus from 'events' to the notion of a 'career'. Child protection is a process in which the outcomes of one stage are inputs to the next. Thus, children may be said to have 'protection careers' comprising linked sequences of decisions made about them. These careers are influenced by children's and families' responses to such decisions, and so may be observed to have distinct stages or episodes. Along the way, many cases are diverted from the protection process but the further a case progresses, the more complicated becomes the means of departure. How many ACPC and agency databases incorporate this longitudinal dimension and with what consequences for decision making?

The effective supervision and training of social workers

Because professionals involved in child protection are influential, it is clear that their competence is more than a matter of simply adhering to rules and following guidance; they need to display sensitivity and discretion combined with forceful curiosity. Three points emphasised in the research are helpful.

HOW EFFECTIVE IS the supervision of child protection professionals?

The researchers found that many inexperienced social workers dealt with extremely difficult situations alone. This has several negative effects: it keeps thresholds for action low; it fails to engage non-resident parents, non-custodial fathers and the wider family; it leads to important issues, such as domestic violence, being ignored.
The quality of supervision affects professional morale. Informal sources of support and the informal ethos of teams were an important influence on the quality of work undertaken.

The diversity of child abuse cases creates anxiety among practitioners. Cases do not fit clear categories, assessment is sometimes inconclusive and prediction remains difficult. Yet the quality of the supervision that social workers received was very variable, and inexperienced staff often had to deal with extremely difficult situations alone. In some instances team-work was inadequate because of staff shortages or lack of resources. If uncertainty and lack of confidence among practitioners are to be prevented from keeping thresholds for action nervously low, the formal and informal sources of professional support need to be monitored and strengthened. Similarly if Part III services are to be used more frequently for abused children and risks are to be taken, professional morale has to be high. Team ethos is a vital ingredient.

Poor case supervision can also confound long-term plans. It led to insufficient support for the main parent or carer (including the non-abusing parent in cases of sexual abuse) during investigations and when protection plans were being implemented, sometimes to the extent that if help was offered they were too hostile or angry to accept it. The situation was worse where other family members were concerned, and there was an almost universal failure to engage non-resident parents and wider relatives in either the enquiry or the protection plan. The tendency to ignore absent, non-resident fathers when decisions about their offspring were being made was particularly regrettable.

Finally, limited training, inadequate supervision and the lack of a supportive peer group reduce awareness of important issues bearing on child abuse. Domestic violence, for example, frequently features in child abuse contexts yet was rarely dealt with as a separate issue in assessment or treatment. A similar myopia hindered discussion about a child's 'family'. The common preoccupation was with the nuclear aspect, which more often than not consisted of a single female parent or involved step-parents, situations where there were frequently specific problems, irrespective of any abuse. On the other hand, the significance of wider patterns of kinship and other sources of emotional support was often overlooked.

Enhancing children's general quality of life

All the evidence discussed so far supports the argument that enhancing a child's wider quality of life increases the likelihood of protection from abuse. Yet, the research also showed that no single strategy could be relied upon to bring about such improvements once abuse had ceased. What might work in one case might even do harm in another. Generalisations about the merits of removing children, expelling abusers and supporting vulnerable families, all of which may be valid options depending on the circumstances, are usually found wanting because of the complexity of individual cases. As Gibbons, Gallagher and other colleagues' study of physically abused children registered ten years previously confirms:

We could find no evidence that children who were legally protected (by care or other orders) did significantly better. Nor did those removed from their abusers, and placed in new permanent or long-term families, have significantly better outcomes than those who remained with their original carers. This still held, even for children who had been in their new families almost from the start of their lives and had not experienced many moves. This may have been due to poor selection of children for placement - although the children in new families had a greater weighting of risk factors than the others, the differences were small - as well as to contemporary policies which interpreted the need for 'permanency' in an over-restrictive way.

These findings also suggest that one cannot guarantee a better quality of parenting simply by moving a child to an apparently non-abusing family. Harmful parenting methods, notably in the use of physical punishment and a generally punitive atmosphere in the home, were found as often in adoptive homes as in natural families - though less frequently in foster homes. Foster carers received social work support which adoptive parents usually lacked, indicating a need for further development of post-adoptive work.

Sexually abused children attending specialist treatment programmes also show only small changes during the first year of intervention. The report on the clinical trial at Great Ormond Street Hospital demonstrates the difficulty. It was expected that the addition of group therapy to a well-established family network treatment would improve the outcomes for sexually abused children and their families. However, Monck and colleagues' comparison of children found that the addition of the group therapy was only as effective as the baseline family work in producing improvement during the year of treatment, at least as rated on five non-clinical standard measures. Clinicians produced more optimistic ratings for the mothers and children who had received the group therapy. Mothers in treatment showed more improvement over the year of study than their children. In Monck and New's later study of sexually abused children referred for treatment to voluntary agency community facilities, neither the children nor their mothers showed significant progress on a series of standardised measures.

Improving effectiveness

Given the difficulties and constraints described, what can be done to improve the situation? A useful way of answering this question is to explore why some difficult cases did well and why some promising candidates fared badly.

Thoburn and colleagues examined the extent to which parents took part in the protection process, as participants or partners. Using criteria based on previous work, they rated each case on the extent to which involvement appeared to be a realistic possibility, classifying the potential for partnership in terms of a

WHAT ARE THE BENEFITS of family support for child protection enquiries?

When family support is being offered, parents find questions about abuse less traumatic and they are more likely to cooperate with professionals. Conference decisions are implemented, care plans are effective and interventions address the wider needs that may have contributed to the abuse. The functions of different parts of the process - investigation, professional meetings, plans and reviews - are clear and correctly focused, and the child is less likely to be re-abused.

When family support is absent, parents are less likely to be aware of what is going on, the child is at risk of drift and decisions are focused on isolated abuse incidents. Resources are too narrowly directed and outcomes for children are worse in areas in addition to abuse and neglect, such as health, education, growth and development and social and family relationships.

'best', 'middle' or 'worst' scenario. The hypothesis that some families and family members would be particularly difficult to engage was not entirely borne out, except in a small number of cases at each end of the continuum. In just over a quarter of 'best scenario' cases, family members were not drawn into the process at all and only a quarter could be said to have participated, whereas a measure of involvement was achieved in 69% of those in the 'worst scenario' cases and 19% actually participated. They concluded:

> whilst failure to work in partnership can sometimes be attributed to aspects of the case itself or characteristics of family members, differences between cases where family members were informed, involved and consulted and those where they were not were almost always attributable to either the agency policy and procedures or the social work practice, or both together.

This finding has considerable implications for children, since greater involvement in the protection process is associated with good outcomes for parents. More importantly, parents' satisfaction with the process was also closely related to a positive outcome for the child, except in the small number of cases where a decision was made to place a young child permanently outside the family.

Scope for improvement was also highlighted in the work of Sharland and colleagues. For a quarter of the children they studied, good prospects were associated with poor practice (but bad prospects accompanied good practice in only 9% of cases). As a result, the situation and achievements of some sexually abused children worsened despite their being good candidates for help. This deterioration was more likely if the abuse was outside the family or if suspicions were not confirmed. These children received no follow-through service and little attempt was made to reconcile the differing perceptions of parents and social workers as to the welfare needs of the child.

The Dartington study came to a similar conclusion, pointing to families who went without any help because there was a failure to provide a welfare service. In the case of 'acutely distressed' families, for example, an over-concern in Section 47 enquiries on questions of maltreatment and a reluctance to consider avenues of family support were frequently detrimental. The variety of Section 17 services available, including recourse to the Social Fund and family therapy, rarely featured in practitioners' discussions. It emerged also that multi-problem families, who were well known to welfare and control agencies, would probably have benefited from a general, cross-agency service. Not only would this strategy satisfy much unmet need – 30 of the 61 children studied still needed help even though the initial suspicions of abuse had not been confirmed – it would also reduce the pressure on the child protection process. Fifty-six per cent of referrals in the study were found to have come from these two types of family.

In demonstrating the benefits for children of emphasising that a continuum exists between child protection, family support and child welfare, the researchers are not suggesting taking unnecessary risks with children's lives. Neither are they suggesting letting abusers off the hook and transferring all the blame on to carers coping in difficult situations. What they are saying is that risks must be taken in order to get a more successful outcome for the child by keeping various avenues of family support firmly in mind when child protection enquiries are underway. This applies to the many cases described in the studies where agreement could have been reached without recourse to the child protection process or where attempts at protection were actually harmful to the child. Child protection can never be completely risk–free but professional anxiety can be reduced by an informed awareness of children's long-term situations.

How can professionals best protect children? Summary points

- Five features of effective practice have been identified; sensitive and informed professional/client relationships; an appropriate balance of power between the key parties; a wide perspective on child abuse; effective supervision and training of social workers; and a determination to enhance the quality of children's lives.

- These conditions were frequently met and many cases reached a satisfactory conclusion. However, relations between clients and professionals were often spoiled by insufficient participation, and a shortage of information for parents. Because professional attitudes to abuse were too restricted, children's wider needs and relevant aspects of family life were neglected. The narrowness of the social work approach was a reflection of poor supervision and training.

- The studies showed that clients suffered whenever professionals became preoccupied with a specific event, ignored the wider context, chose the wrong 'career avenue' for the child or excluded the family from the enquiry.

- The 'secondary' adjustment needs of the families and children were rarely addressed by practitioners. Whenever proper attention was paid to these needs there were general benefits.

- Protection is best achieved by building on the existing strengths of the child's living situation, rather than expecting miracles from isolated and spasmodic interventions.

- Respect for family rights can also contribute to a child's protection. Basic child-care principles need to be combined with specialist work if the long-term interests of children are to be enhanced.

- Specialist treatments, at least in sexual abuse cases, appear to enhance maternal understanding and skills and reduce maternal distress, at least in the short-term. Children, however, benefit less.

Conclusions

At the time of the Colwell, Beckford and Cleveland Inquiries, all major scandals, public debate about child abuse was widespread, yet there was little empirical evidence to support the various arguments. The gaps in knowledge were identified in terms of the definition and diagnosis of child maltreatment, the response of protection agencies when suspected abuse came to light and the most effective form of intervention. At moments of crisis, discussions tend to focus on moral questions - the rights of parents or the trauma of children - or on legal matters -whether professionals are too intrusive or have sufficient powers. The demand was clear - for more children to be protected more effectively. To satisfy these concerns, the guidance *Working Together* was issued in 1988 and subsequently revised in 1991. A period of relative calm ensued when cool, dispassionate research once more found its place.

Whereas previously there was a dearth of reliable evidence on child protection and child abuse, there are now over 40 major works from which to choose. If literature from abroad and the plethora of practice manuals and polemics published in the last decade are also taken into account, it might be concluded that research has complicated rather than clarified the issue. However, important messages for policy and practice have emerged. This overview has summarised the principal messages from 17 studies in a Department of Health research programme and three complementary research investigations. Where necessary, reference has been made to other works.

The overview began with questions of definition. What is child abuse? What is meant by the term child protection? It then went on to describe the protection process and encouraged professionals to view their contribution in the context of other work on behalf of children. As would be expected from such an extensive scrutiny, considerable outcome evidence has been provided to show what happens to children who are maltreated, what styles of intervention work and what happens to parents suspected of abusing their offspring. It is hoped that such information will help improve knowledge and practice; indeed, there follows a set of exercises designed to encourage professionals to collect evidence and learn from their own evidence.

It has been demonstrated that any potentially abusive *incident* has to be seen in *context* before the extent of its harm can be assessed and appropriate inter-ventions agreed. An important part of the context is evidence about the likely effects of maltreatment on the child, that is to say the *outcome* of abuse. Many of the studies reviewed have provided such information and show that, with the exception of a few severe assaults and some sexual maltreatment, long-term difficulties for children seldom follow from a single abusive event; rather they are more likely to be a consequence of living in an unfavourable environment, particularly one which is low in warmth and high in criticism.

Except in a few extreme cases where the decision is clear cut, as a society we have to decide which of the several million potentially harmful situations that occur each year require intervention. A threshold is drawn across behaviours which ordinarily happen and some, by virtue of their severity, context or duration, demand that professionals enquire into the situation to see what remedies are needed. Other thresholds are drawn at subsequent stages of the child protection process; at the first involvement of parents, when calling a protection meeting, convening a full conference or placing the child's name on the protection register. In deciding whether to act, professionals are influenced by legal/moral concerns which lay out the obligations of statutory authorities. But there are also practical considerations, not least the parents' willingness to co-operate and the child's reaction to the process. As well as stressing the value of outcome evidence, the research has pointed out the importance of parental and child perspectives when deciding what action to take.

Psychological evidence suggests that while children suffer in an environment of low warmth and high criticism, the intervention of professionals in these situations is seldom necessary or helpful. If, however, family problems endure, some external support, perhaps using Section 17 services, will be required to ensure that the health and development of the child is not significantly impaired. If the child's fraught situation endures, then he or she is likely to suffer significant harm and may need to be looked after away from home. There are, in addition, a small proportion of cases in which the abuse is extreme and will not be reduced by family support alone. For children who have been grossly injured or sexually abused, swift child rescue, sometimes using emergency powers, will be necessary. However, the research evidence suggests that, for the majority of cases, the need of the child and family is more important than the abuse or, put another way, the general family context is more important than any abusive event within it. This message applies when defining maltreatment, designing interventions or assessing outcomes.

Thus, in addition to the considerable burden of *child protection* work, professionals also offer *family support* and provide *child welfare* for the small proportion who live away from home. For a child-care system to be effective, some overlap between these services is inevitable. But the research studies have questioned whether the balance between child protection and the range of supports and interventions available to professionals is correct. This is an issue Area Child Protection Committees and professionals associated with this group must constantly raise about services in their region.

The research studies suggest that too much of the work undertaken comes under the banner of child protection. In the diagram describing the child protection process, first described on page 28, child protection work - frequently thought of as investigations rather than enquiries - was seen to dominate. A more useful perspective is offered in the diagram over the page. Here, much early work is viewed as an enquiry to establish whether the child in need might benefit from services. In only a proportion of cases will the child protection processes be called into play - the outcome of which will be family support or, in a minority of situations, child welfare for those living away from home.

Such an approach to children in need would help rebut the criticism that many investigations are undertaken, many families are visited and case conferences

HAVE PROFESSIONALS ACHIEVED the correct balance between child protection, family support and child welfare?

When faced with a needy family, professionals have several available options from which to choose. They might undertake a *child protection* enquiry; they could offer *family support* services to bolster the household's defences; or they could assess the situation and provide *child welfare* services, for example, a place in a community or foster home. There is a tendency to think of these avenues as either/or when, in fact, the *Children Act*, 1989 allows for several possibilities to be kept open.

For example, a Section 47 enquiry - the child protection route - is to establish whether any action to safeguard or promote the child's welfare is needed. The most likely form of action will be services under Section 17 of the Act - the family support route - including, if necessary, local authority accommodation and respite care. In exceptional circumstances, emergency action under Part V of the 1989 legislation may be required or the child may have to be looked after for an extended period - the child welfare route. All of these options are available at the moment abuse is suspected and best outcomes follow from making the routes complementary rather than exclusive.

This said, at the time the research was undertaken, the balance between services was unsatisfactory. The stress upon child protection investigations and not enquiries, and the failure to follow through interventions with much needed family support prevented professionals from meeting the needs of children and families.

called but that, in the end, little support is offered to the family. In such situations, it is unsurprising that participants become angry, alienated and bewildered. Furthermore, the children are not helped and a chunk of valuable child-care resource has been consumed with little apparent benefit.

A more balanced service for vulnerable children would encourage professionals to take a wider view. There would be efforts to work alongside families rather than disempower them, to raise their self-esteem rather than reproach families, to promote family relationships where children have their needs met, rather than leave untreated families with an unsatisfactory parenting style. The focus would be on the overall needs of children rather than a narrow concentration on the alleged incident.

An approach based on the *process* of Section 47 enquiries and the *provision* of Section 17 services (including those for children looked after away from home), might well shift the emphasis in child protection work more towards family support. This, in turn, might encourage local authorities to review the type of Section 17 services provided and to consider how well these are matched to their priority cases. Provision will include both universal preventative services and specific interventions for the multiply deprived families commonly subject to Section 47 enquiries.

Getting this balance right at national, local and family level will still depend on how the moral, legal and pragmatic questions that influence thresholds are answered at any given moment; but, increasingly, outcome information from research, from organisations such as the Audit Commission, from inspections and evaluations and from local authorities will play a part, as will consumer perspectives on which interventions are most appropriate.

As child protection services evolve, they need to be continuously assessed and reviewed. The message from the 20 studies is that decisions about children in need are, to some extent, socially constructed and that the same need may require different inputs in different historical eras. Post-Cleveland the need was for an ordered protection service; in ten years time the need might well be for family support and protection. If policy and practice changes are to follow from this round of research, it should be to reconsider the balance of services and alter the way in which professionals are perceived by parents accused of abusing or neglecting their offspring.

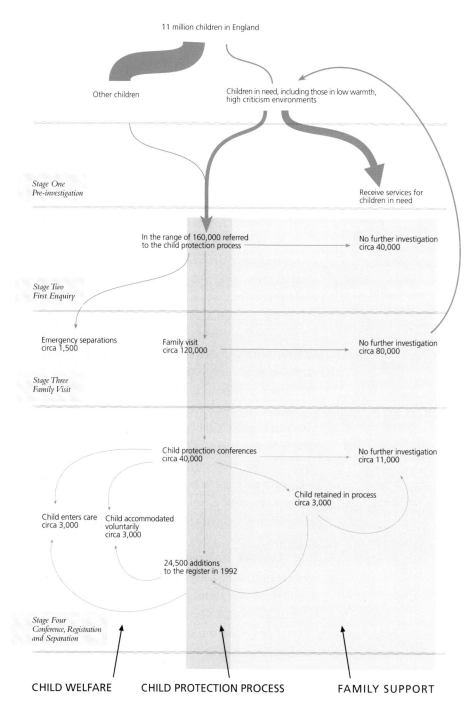

11 million children in England

Other children

Children in need, including those in low warmth, high criticism environments

*Stage One
Pre-investigation*

Receive services for children in need

In the range of 160,000 referred to the child protection process

No further investigation circa 40,000

*Stage Two
First Enquiry*

Emergency separations circa 1,500

Family visit circa 120,000

No further investigation circa 80,000

*Stage Three
Family Visit*

Child protection conferences circa 40,000

No further investigation circa 11,000

Child retained in process circa 3,000

Child enters care circa 3,000

Child accommodated voluntarily circa 3,000

24,500 additions to the register in 1992

*Stage Four
Conference, Registration
and Separation*

CHILD WELFARE   CHILD PROTECTION PROCESS   FAMILY SUPPORT

Summaries of the research reports

The following summaries were prepared with the authors themselves with an eye to identifying the main findings that are relevant to professional practice. Less attention is given to research design and methodology in each case, but information of that kind can be found in David Gough's review of the literature, *Child Abuse Interventions*. Those wanting more details about the research or to question in greater depth the reliability of the findings should turn to the publications.

The table below is an attempt to show which publications are the most relevant to the themes and practice issues described in the preceding essay.

Study	What is meant by abuse?	The child protection process	How effective is the child protection process?	How can professionals best protect children?
Cleaver and Freeman		✓		✓
Farmer and Owen		✓		✓
Ghate and Spencer	✓			
Gibbons, Gallagher, Bell and Gordon			✓	✓
Gibbons, Conroy and Bell		✓	✓	
Hallett and Birchall		✓	✓	
La Fontaine	✓			
Monck and New			✓	✓
Monck, Sharland, Bentovim *et al*		✓	✓	
Sharland, Jones, Aldgate *et al*		✓		
Smith and Grocke	✓			
Smith, Bee, Heverin and Nobes	✓			
Thoburn, Lewis and Shemmings		✓		✓
Kelly, Regan and Burton	✓			
The Research Team (Belfast)	✓			
Waterhouse		✓		✓

Parental Perspectives in Cases of Suspected Child Abuse

Hedy Cleaver and Pam Freeman, Dartington Social Research Unit

This report contains a discussion of the historical and cultural context of child abuse, a description of the problems of gaining research access to the child protection system, and detailed studies of a series of cases based on interviews with professionals and family members caught up in a child abuse investigation. There is also a description of the use of 'operational perspectives' as a means of understanding how agreement in such cases is negotiated.

At the time the studies were commissioned there was concern not only that vulnerable families might be harmed by the child protection process itself, but that for some the mere fact of having been under suspicion could be damaging. The Dartington study sought to understand the experience of families caught up in the web of an investigation. It also sought to demonstrate how the perceptions of parents and those of the professionals they encountered in such cases influenced subsequent events. The research had two main strands, a survey of 583 child protection cases in one local authority and a detailed study in two authorities of 30 families caught up in the early stages of an inquiry.

From the first part of the study it emerged that many allegations were not substantiated and that in the majority of instances where children had been abused the damage was generally regarded as having been minor. Fewer than a third of the children eventually had their names placed on the child protection register and most of those remained at home. Even for those children separated from their families, reunion remained the most likely outcome, unless they had suffered very serious abuse.

Certain factors seemed common to all cases. Some form of family reconstitution or major change in adult membership had generally taken place and any man recently arrived in the household was very likely to be the focus of the suspicion. Mothers and fathers were equally likely to come under suspicion as perpetrators of physical abuse, but in cases of neglect and emotional abuse, it was more commonly mothers. Where the the allegation concerned sexual abuse, men, most frequently fathers, were the most likely suspects.

The chances of a child's name being added to the protection register were stronger when social services, police, hospitals or probation rather than health visitors or GPs were involved in the initial referral. Schools were an important source of information but a less coherent influence upon registration. Likelihood of registration was again greater if someone with a record of child abuse or violence was present in the family, if sexual abuse was alleged, or if the family was well known to social services and considered generally to be turbulent.

From the detailed study, during which the fortunes of 30 families and their 61 children were followed for two years, it was clear that the impact of suspicion tended to be worst among parents who had been unaware of the gathering disquiet and had no previous dealings with social services. They felt invaded and humiliated; they rejected anything that was insinuated against them, but fretted that the confrontation was bound to lead to the removal of the child. In such cases it was doubly difficult for social workers to tell the distress of the innocent from the remorse of the guilty.

Parents not only had to cope with suspicion directed against them from outside. Mothers were inclined to suspect others in the family, partners resented the disclosures of mothers or stepchildren, siblings were likely to play down the incident and inveigh against the publicity; supposed victims would retreat into denial rather than endure more scrutiny. For everyone there were

In the wake of suspicion, one child in five moved out of the family home (usually to the shelter of relatives), one family in three moved house and a similar number experienced the arrival or departure of a key figure, usually the husband or co-habitee. These structural changes were almost all for the better and, as living situations improved, so did the physical health of families. On the other hand, there was a marked deterioration in intimate family relationships, particularly between adults. Marital stress increased and in nearly half the cases the central relationship collapsed during the two year follow-up period.

Schools emerged as a significant agent of referral and, once the child was registered, they were in a good position to monitor progress. However, schools varied greatly in their ability to cope with abuse problems. For example, because headteachers and those with special responsibility for abuse and pastoral care differed in their handling of confidentiality, it was not unusual for classroom teachers in some schools to be unaware of those children whose names were placed on the protection register or for whom concern was growing.

Structural factors in schools were also a hindrance. Teachers hesitated to set the abuse procedures in motion because they were so disturbing to classroom routine. The process violated the trust of parents, disrupted the child-teacher relationship and was likely to come to the uncomprehending notice of other children. It seemed doubtful whether many classrooms were capable of providing that asylum of compassion that abused children needed, particularly bearing in mind that those most at risk were not particularly loveable on other criteria: they were frequently in trouble, and, possibly conveniently from the school's point of view, frequently absent.

differences between what they felt and what they admitted to feeling. A mood of recrimination sometimes beset the home. On the other side of the domestic divide, professionals, overburdened with abuse investigations or pre-occupied with other problems, might easily lose sight of how violating the procedure could seem. It had an inbuilt momentum which, unless reined in by a sensitive social worker, aggravated parents' feelings of vulnerability.

To understand the forces at work behind this curtain of anxieties, the researchers identified key moments in an enquiry such as when suspicion moved into the public domain, when a formal accusation was made, when professionals met and when fresh evidence came to light. At such moments, it was argued, a parent's attitude to the child protection procedures was most likely to be amenable to change. Much depended on certain psychological and social influences on an individual's view of his or her situation: psychological influences might include personality, previous experience and motivation; social influences included the power relationship between parent and professional, the way suspicion entered the public domain and who confronted the parents. To describe these conditioning aspects of perception, the term 'operational perspective' was used. It was argued that if an investigation was to have a successful outcome, the operational perspectives of parents and professionals must be permitted or, better, assisted to converge.

The evidence from the case studies was that hostility might moderate with time, but wariness of professional intrusion was likely to endure. This was an obstacle to progress, because so many families continued to need help with problems far removed from any issue of abuse. Furthermore, the accusation sometimes acted as a detonator to that volatile mixture of love, hate and indifference which held families together. That said, there was much else to suggest that the child protection system did succeed in protecting the majority of children at risk. It might be impossible to protect the few from occasional violence, rejection and indifference, but in many cases even the awareness of external scrutiny was a sufficient check on the temperature of family life.

There was plainly a fine balance to be struck between the benefits of intervention and its potential for doing harm. In many cases there was little evidence of abuse and professional attention rapidly moved elsewhere, but an accusation that was all in the day's work for a health visitor or a social worker could leave catastrophe in its wake. The disintegration of marital relationships that was recorded, the movement of family members and the relocation of children were high prices to pay for a bruise or for the witnessing by children of an unsuitable video.

There was ambiguity, too, when outcomes were viewed from the perspective of the social worker. In some cases persistent professional anxiety eventually resulted in an allegation being substantiated and the legal process intervening; in other cases simmering concern enabled a social worker to re-evaluate a case and to appreciate the efforts made by mothers in particular to cope with less pressing problems. The lesson was in this vein: few protection plans that stopped short of removing a child to a place of safety could guarantee physical security, but opportunities to improve professional–parental relationships, which in 70 per cent of cases led to a successful case outcome, were relatively common. In establishing the various thresholds of child protection, it was therefore especially important to consider where to fix the threshold of concern beyond which it became right to intervene in the intimate lives of families. Such decisons were being made at the point of referral, when social workers paid an informal visit and when the child or parent was interviewed. As things stood, anyone in regular contact with children, however uncertain or untrained in abuse matters, had the power to inflict child protection procedures on parents. For lack of any sensitively drawn procedural guideline, it seemed that professional anxiety was keeping thresholds for action low.

Parents' attitudes to the social work system were soured if they found out that in the early stages of an investigation questions had been asked behind their backs. But chaotic families already well supported by social workers might as easily be approached without any need to raise the spectre of a specific allegation. It was estimated that this simple strategy would help in more than one incident in three. The thornier problems occurred among those families unused to social work interventions or where, unbeknown to close partners or friends, family members had a history of child abuse. In such situations, wherever the threshold of intervention lay, the social worker was unlikely to be a welcome guest.

Child Protection Practice: Private Risks and Public Remedies
Decision Making, Intervention and Outcome in Child Protection Work

Elaine Farmer and Morag Owen, University of Bristol

This study includes historical analysis of society's response to child maltreatment, descriptions of the investigative process and methods of intervention over a 20 month follow-up period. Material is drawn from interviews with professionals and family members in cases involving different forms of abuse and neglect. There are accounts of case conferences from the viewpoints of professionals and family members, and descriptions of categories of case outcome and the links with different kinds of intervention.

There was a tendency for early child protection research to be preoccupied with the identification and investigation of children at risk. One of the aims of the Bristol study was to increase understanding of what made subsequent professional action effective. The team worked in two local authorities observing case conferences and collecting evidence from parents, children and supervising social workers. Because their research was prospective, it became possible to assess how well cases turned out in the light of a decision making process that had been witnessed at first hand.

In all, 120 case conferences were observed and an analysis of their structure and of the ways in which decisions were made is at the heart of the team's report. From the large sample they extracted a follow-up group of 44 registered children whose cases provided the basis for the detailed part of the study. In addition, interviews were conducted in a third local authority which had a large minority ethnic population in order to draw out some of the issues involved in child protection work with families from minority ethnic groups.

It was very common for parents to feel threatened by the police presence at case conferences and for them to say they had not been informed about it. Regardless of the composition of the group, parents often felt that there were simply too many people in attendance.

Many black families did not have access to much-needed services. Even after registration this situation often continued, partly because of a lack of ethnically appropriate resources. Good racial matching was helpful, but there were some occasions when it was done crudely, with the result that workers from very different minority cultures wrongly assumed they understood the family's situation.

In addition, issues such as gender and class were of great importance in the allocation of workers. Where there was successful matching across the dimensions of race, gender and ethnicity, parental satisfaction was higher and the progress of the children correspondingly better.

The investigation stage was very stressful for professionals and family members. For over a third of the parents it was the first that they had heard of the allegation and many experienced shock, confusion, anger and the onset of profound feelings of loss. Professionals often underestimated the impact of the allegations and of the investigation on parents and had a tendency to view their immediate reactions as immutable. In particular, the withdrawal of support from non-abusing parents adversely affected their ability to assist in their children's recovery and could delay the return of those children who had been removed.

Several patterns emerged by which an assessment of risk was made at case conferences. In the first, worries about the child were treated as cumulative; in the second, the likelihood of the situation deteriorating or of an incident of abuse being repeated was the pivotal concern; in the third, the focus was on specific parental behaviour from which abuse or neglect was considered to result. A fourth pattern, which took account of the dynamics of the family and the possible underlying cause of the abuse, was found more rarely, so that for the most part the methods of assessment were felt to be less than adequate as a basis for long-term care planning. In over a third of the protection plans formulated at the first case conferences important aspects of the child's future protection were overlooked. The preoccupation with risk meant there was simply too little time - nine minutes on average - to consider the needs of the family or what should be done.

Factors closely related to the decision to register a child were the perceived severity of the abuse or neglect, the existence of secondary concerns (for example evidence of neglect in a household where physical or sexual abuse was suspected), and the prior involvement of the family with other treatment agencies. Whenever mothers were regarded as responsible for abuse, the children were more likely to be registered.

Since in the aftermath of the case conference the majority of the parents (70%) were unhappy with the treatment they had received up to that point, social workers were expected to carry out much of what had been decided in trying circumstances. In some cases there was active resistance, in others a strategy of minimum compliance. Matters did tend to improve, however. For two-fifths of the families in the intensive study the hurt of the investigation was still felt 20 months later, but most of those who had been alienated in the early stages became better disposed. Those social workers who kept in constructive contact both with the child and other family members were highly valued, and this kind of co-operation contributed greatly to a good outcome. In many cases where there was serious friction at the outset, a change of social worker was found to be the key to a better relationship and a fresh start.

There was a close link between the adequacy of the initial child protection plans and the child's safety. In eight out of ten cases where the plan was considered sound the child was protected, and in half the cases where the initial plan was considered lacking a child was subsequently re-abused or neglected.

Women often turned to professional agencies in order to get help either for themselves or as a way of coping with the behaviour of men with whom they were living. If, as a result, child protection procedures were set in motion they frequently felt unfairly condemned. The problem became extreme if mothers sought help because they suspected abuse or because of child management difficulties, since they themselves were quite likely to come under suspicion. Such experiences spoke for a widespread assumption in most cases of neglect and emotional abuse that mothers were responsible for faults in the care of children. It also accounted for their reluctance to seek help.

Questionable treatment of single mothers was also a feature of case management after registration. Those whose children were registered stood a higher chance of having children permanently removed; in addition, mothers whose male partners sexually abused their children tended to be treated as secondary perpetrators, but should they demonstrate that they were able to protect their children from their erstwhile partners, their reward was usually to find the case was quickly closed, leaving them with the full responsibility of coping with the aftermath of abuse without the support of social services.

The protection plan had the most enduring influence when the social worker was new to the case at the time of registration. There was also a tendency for early weaknesses to be accentuated; once a pattern of case management was established it was usually endorsed at subsequent reviews and even major flaws failed to be identified.

By the end of the study most of the sexually abused children were living with a non-abusing parent. Half had received individual counselling and spoke about it as something which they valued highly. In contrast, children who received no counselling or any other direct help had adjusted markedly less well and in cases where it had been assumed that because the perpetrator was out of the household mothers could protect their children, social work intervention often ended much too quickly. The difficulties of children and their mothers deepened when assistance was withdrawn.

Twenty months after registration, two-fifths of the children who had suffered physical abuse, neglect or emotional abuse were being looked after away from home. In some circumstances children who stayed at home were exposed to serious continuing risks, for example if social workers had developed high thresholds of tolerance for the parenting standards of families well-known to them.

Although physical injuries were inflicted in equal numbers by father figures and lone mothers, social work focused almost exclusively on mothers. In three out of five of the cases where children had suffered physical abuse, neglect or emotional abuse the mothers were also subject to violence by their male partners. The associated risks and the fact that many of the children witnessed violence to their mothers was given little attention by professionals. Yet domestic violence was a feature of most of the cases with the worst outcomes.

When the cases involving minority ethnic families were compared with those in the sample as a whole it was noted that a high number of investigations ended in uncertainty and this gave the ensuing intervention a diffuse focus. The stresses experienced by parents during the investigation and initial case conference were compounded by language differences and cultural misunderstandings. Successful matching across the dimensions of gender and ethnicity as well as race contributed to parent satisfaction.

Case outcome was evaluated on three fronts: whether the children had been protected, their general welfare had been enhanced and the needs of parents or carers met. There was progress on every front in just 23% of cases. Among the largest group (27%) some progress was made in child protection and welfare terms but the needs of the main carers were neglected. In a third group (21%) the children were protected without any other progress having been made. Most of these were cases of sexual abuse. Often the alleged abuser was out of the household, the mother was being relied on to protect the child and the case had been speedily closed. Among 11%, in the absence of a co-operative relationship with parents, the agency concentrated on monitoring and providing services to the child. In consequence, there was some

Physical injuries were inflicted in roughly equal proportions by father figures and single mothers, but social work focused almost exclusively on mothers. As telling was the finding that in more than half the cases where children had suffered physical abuse, neglect or emotional abuse, there was other violence in the household usually directed against women by men, yet the fact that so many children frequently witnessed violence to their mothers was paid too little attention. Domestic violence was a feature of most of the cases in which both children and parents fared worst

improvement in the child's welfare, but the child was not protected and little was done for the parents. In all such cases the focus of agency attention was the mother; beyond reach in the shadows stood an abusive husband or co-habitee. In the group with the worst outcomes (11%), the children were not protected, nor were their needs or those of their parents met. There were high levels of violence in such families; parenting standards were poor and the behaviour of the children was disturbed. There was a lack of clarity about how the families should be handled and little assistance for the social worker had been provided by the initial conferences or reviews. The problems in these families were regarded as deeply entrenched, low levels of service were provided and efforts to monitor the children's safety were not sustained. The remaining seven per cent were mostly cases of neglect in which some fairly slow general progress was made.

After 20 months, 70 per cent of the children were protected, most commonly by separation of the abuser from the abused child, and in 68 per cent of cases the welfare needs of the child were adequately addressed. However, in only 30 per cent of cases were the needs of the primary carer reasonably well met. The team came to the conclusion that the priority given to child protection was too frequently allowed to obscure the broader developmental and treatment needs of abused children and the severity of their parents' disadvantage. Yet it was clear that deficits in the services offered in these areas could affect the well-being and the long-term protection of the child.

The Prevalence of Child Sexual Abuse in Britain: A Feasibility Study for a Large Scale National Survey of the General Population
Deborah Ghate and Liz Spencer, Social and Community Planning Research

This study considers the problems of undertaking prevalence studies of child sexual abuse. Issues of definition, sampling, response rates and information quality are discussed, along with ethical and procedural matters.

This SCPR study was designed to assess the feasibility of carrying out a national survey of the prevalence, contexts and circumstances of sexually abusive experiences in childhood. It set out to evaluate a number of methodological, procedural and ethical issues, including case definition; context, approach and presentation; response rates and bias; the size, type and composition of the sample; problems associated with memory and recall; the preparation and training of interviewers, and administrative methods.

Because of the delicate nature of the work, a developmental approach was adopted, each phase building on the lessons and findings of the last. First there was a familiarisation stage, involving consultation with professionals, practitioners and academics and a review of the literature. Next there was a programme of unstructured interviews with survivors of sexual abuse, who were recruited through counselling organisations and who between them were able to speak of a wide range of experience varying from chronic intra-familial abuse to isolated incidents of abuse by strangers. Semi-structured interviews were then used as a basis on which to develop questionnaire modules. Finally, structured interviews were conducted using a fully developed questionnaire.

The study demonstrated convincingly that a large scale national survey would indeed be feasible. Anxieties about poor response to the survey as a whole or to particular questions, proved to be largely unfounded. The response rate to the last pre-pilot was in the region of 71%.

However, it was clear that the initial method of approach, sensitive interviewing technique and careful structuring of questions were vitally important considerations if the public was to participate fully and those who had sexually abusive childhood experiences to recount were not to be left in distress.

To maximise reporting, it was concluded that any pre-definition of types of abuse was to be avoided and that a broad approach covering the range of sexual experience to be encountered before the age of 16 should be adopted. By that means it would be possible to apply definitions later, in accordance with flexible criteria and a range of specialist definitions.

It was found to be possible to gather explicit information on various aspects of childhood sexual experiences using face-to-face interviewing methods. Where the sexual content of experience was being discussed and the need for sensitivity was greatest, show-card techniques proved to be valuable. Self-completion methods were considered more prone to error and more likely to produce superficial and simplistic responses.

Another key finding was that memories of childhood experiences of abuse were unlikely to be uncovered by a single phase of data collection. Some people remembered incidents some time after they parted company with the interviewer. In keeping with what was at that time regarded as a tendency for abusive experiences to be repressed, there were strong suggestions that a second round of data collection was required to record recollections triggered by the first interview. Such findings endorsed the need to provide post-interview support and information for respondents.

Development After Physical Abuse in Early Childhood: A Follow-up Study of Children on Protection Registers

Jane Gibbons, Bernard Gallagher, Caroline Bell and David Gordon, University of East Anglia

This study contains detailed information about the development of children nine to ten years after physical abuse, the context in which physical abuse occurs, events in the lives of abused children and their effects on outcomes, family relationships and children's views of themselves and their worlds. It describes the effects of placement in permanent substitute families and of protective services on children's outcomes.

This study describes the longer-term consequences of physical abuse in early childhood by making a comparison between the outcomes of children who at a given moment were considered to be in need of protection with another group of otherwise similar children whose childhood experience might be said to have been unremarkable. Jane Gibbons and her colleagues reasoned that those working in the child protection system often had to take decisions that were bound to have a devastating effect on family life, when still not much was known about what actually happened to the children whose lives were changed by such intervention. An important test was to determine the extent to which children exposed to and protected by social work might be said to have developed similarly to those who were not.

The research team also wanted to discover if children suffered long-term serious damage as a direct consequence of physical abuse and whether any setbacks they experienced were the result of the deprived social circumstances in which they grew up. Similarly, they hoped to be able to evaluate the progress of children parted from their families and placed in new domestic surroundings.

The comparison was made by identifying 170 children in two areas whose names when under five had, nine or ten years previously, been put on protection registers operated by the NSPCC. Each child was paired with another who attended the same school, lived in the same neighbourhood and was a match for gender and age, but who had no connection with child protection services. Various aspects of the well-being of both groups were assessed including growth, intellectual development, how parents and teacher rated their behaviour, and how they themselves described any friendship problems or experience of anxiety or depression.

Abused children were more likely to show behaviour problems at home and school, had greater difficulty with friendships and scored lower on certain cognitive tests. Their families were poorer. They were more commonly headed by a lone parent and they tended to move house more often. On the basis of this assessment, it was calculated that about one in five of the children who had been abused could be said to have fared generally well, twice as many quite poorly, with the remainder somewhere in between. By the same reckoning, twice as many in the comparison group had developed fairly happily.

At a subtler level the picture was less clear. When the attempt was made to ascribe the circumstances in which certain children now found themselves to an aspect of their lives at the time they were mistreated, no strong pattern of connections could be established. Whenever neglect came into the frame of reference the outcome tended to be worse, but it seemed generally to be the case that so much had happened in the intervening period and so much of it by chance that no basis for prediction was to be relied upon.

However, there was evidence that a combination of different kinds of abuse or of abuse and neglect together tended to make the longer-term outlook worse, as probably did persistent abuse. Therefore, it could be said that when physical abuse was an isolated event, when there was no sign of associated neglect or suspected sexual abuse and when the family climate was not generally violent, the outlook for a child was relatively good. But the researchers found that even so tentative a judgement as this needed to be treated with caution: there was nothing to suggest for instance that injury was by itself an important factor; on the contrary, some children at risk of abuse who had never been physically hurt showed signs of more severe depression and they had fared no better in any other respect.

At a minimum estimate a fifth of the abused children experienced further physical abuse and five per cent some sexual abuse after their names were placed on the child protection register, but no link was found between those later incidents and any longer-term consequence. Other events in a child's life

The researchers attempted to compare aspects of family life, such as predictability, reliability and warmth. Children were asked, 'Some kids almost always know how their parents will react to something they've done, but other kids really can't tell how parents will react. Which kids are more like you?' Children with poor outcomes were significantly more likely to see their parents' reactions as unpredictable.

Children were asked questions about how readily available their parents were to them, how much they were to be counted on and whether they kept their promises. The abused children were more likely to see their parents as very busy and not having much time for them. They were more likely to say their fathers did not keep their promises.

The warmth and closeness of children's relations with their parents were tested by questions about whether children talked to parents about things that were troubling them, how much they were praised and encouraged by parents and how parents showed they were fond of them.

In general, children who felt their parents praised and appreciated them tended also to feel their parents had time to spend with them, that the parents kept a check on their activities and that they were fair. Being a good parent from the child's point of view did not seem to mean letting a child do as he or she liked. Reliability and predictability emerged as important qualities for parents to cultivate.

normally considered to be significant did not seem to make any predictable difference to the way things turned out. For example, frequent changes of carer or address did not necessarily do harm.

Against expectations, what emerged was a strong relationship between the well-being of the children in the study and the style of parenting they were currently experiencing. Children in both groups whose parents appeared more critical and readier to punish them, had more behaviour problems, were more inclined to be depressed and had greater difficulty making and keeping friends. There was clear evidence that the children who had been abused were more likely to have been on the receiving end of such treatment. Their parents or carers tended to be beset by worse personal problems themselves and less satisfied with any social services support they received. In such households there was more likely to be violence between the adult partners.

Other findings were more surprising still. In the years that had elapsed since they were registered, over three-quarters of the abused children had known a loss of or change in parent and nearly one in three was in long-term or permanent substitute care. For the majority, the experience of substitute care had greatly improved their social status and there were measurable gains in their physical growth and vocabulary, but in terms of their behaviour and mental well-being there was no evidence of general advantage. Furthermore, in contradiction to the weight of evidence in other studies, those who had been adopted had as many behaviour and friendship problems as those who remained with natural parents. Children in long-term foster care tended to show fewer of these difficulties and were less depressed than adopted children.

It appeared that adoptive parents, the majority of whose children had come to them as toddlers, were not always using the most sensitive methods of child-rearing. They tended to be more punitive and to resort more readily to just those parenting styles associated with poorer outcomes. Adoptive parents also tended to have more problems of their own and to be more depressed than foster carers. They often had to deal with children whose behaviour was difficult and disturbed but, unlike foster carers, they seldom received professional support and so felt more isolated. In the same vein, there was some suggestion that more intensive and durable social work contact was of great benefit to children who remained with their own parents, and that, in their case, a useful package of services should include psychiatric treatment for a parent and support from a voluntary agency or attendance at a family centre.

On the whole, the data accumulated by the study pointed away from the conclusion that physical abuse in early life had a direct effect on children's development. It seemed rather that physical abuse was in some cases an important sign of a number of other generally damaging circumstances, in particular of a harshly punitive, less reliable and less warmly involved style of parenting. The findings suggested that whenever physical abuse was uncovered in a family, attention needed to be paid to the way parents generally dealt with their children and to the usual temperature of family life.

Operating the Child Protection System: A Study of Child Protection Practices in English Local Authorities

Jane Gibbons, Sue Conroy and Caroline Bell, University of East Anglia

This report includes a discussion of the variation in national statistics of children on child protection registers, and describes the results of a postal survey of operational practices in England. There is a description of the characteristics of referred families and a close study of the filters by which cases leave the system or children's names are added to the protection registers.

The study compared the child protection system to a fine-mesh net, in which were caught a quantity of tiddlers as well as marketable fish. It would be better if the small fry were not caught up, but since no rules existed about the exact size of the fish to be caught or, consequently, the correct size of the mesh, each fleet must set its own limits.

Child protection registers came into being in 1974 as part of a package of measures meant to improve inter-agency co-operation in the wake of the death of Maria Colwell. Almost from the outset they appeared to be used to a varying extent by local professionals and often to serve different purposes, so that by 1988, when new Government guidance was published, it had to be underlined that they were not to be regarded as a record of abuse, nor as an instrument by which cases could be ranked, but were intended to provide a central record only of those children who at any moment might be considered to be in need of an inter-agency protection plan.

Commissioned before the *Children Act, 1989* guidelines came into effect, this study was designed to discover how great was the variation in the numbers of children on registers in similar local authorities and to what extent discrepancies in professional practice might influence decisions about whether or not to register a child.

First, it emerged from a national survey that variation was most noticeable in the criteria used to decide whether child protection procedures were warranted in a particular case and in the actual headings under which children were registered. So, in 1990 in Calderdale, for instance, the percentage categorised as 'neglect' was nil, but on the Isle of Wight the figure was 38%; for physical abuse the figure varied between 7% in Cleveland and 64% in Hackney; for sexual abuse from 3% in Wandsworth to 34% in Wolverhampton. In Trafford the rate for sexual abuse per thousand children under 18 was 0.1; in Nottinghamshire it was 18 times higher, and everywhere there seemed to be uncertainty about how to make proper use of the category of 'grave concern' – so much so that a few Area Child Protection Committees had already taken a decision not to use it.

One explanation for the variation lay in the lack of scientific diagnosis. A case of child maltreatment could not be isolated by looking for a series of symptoms, only by applying judgements to do with ideas about goodness or illness that reflected the values and opinions of different cultures even at a very local level. In another direction, there was clearly a link between poverty, poor housing, racial conflict and the stresses which sometimes resulted in parents mistreating their children, and, again, depending on the locality, the more general tone of policy making could be significant. Consequently, areas with high rates of registered children tended also to have high rates of children in care and a large amount of day nursery provision, reflecting variations in local cultures. In some areas it was possible that the figures had simply been distorted by failure to inform the central register of the results of case conferences. That said, nowhere was the register's value as a central record and as a fulcrum for monitoring and review disputed, and in the majority of cases the system was found to be working well.

To find out more about why local authorities with similar mixtures of population should have very different registration rates eight local authorities - four inner and two outer London boroughs and two counties - were selected

Six out of seven children who entered the system at referral were filtered out of it without needing to be placed on a child protection register. In a high proportion (44% of those actually investigated) the investigations led to no action at all. There was no intervention to protect the child nor was any other family support service provided. In only 4% of all referrals were children removed from home under a legal order during the investigation.

Minutes of initial protection conferences were usually lengthy documents, but few contained any formal statement about unresolved child protection issues that made an inter-agency plan necessary. They usually listed the elements of the plan but it was often unclear how the plan related to the risks.

Some 44% of referrals were for suspected physical injury, 28% for suspected sexual abuse and 25% for neglect. Only 3% related to emotional abuse without other forms of maltreatment. Fewer than one child in 20 referred for physical abuse suffered serious injury.

In order of frequency, referrals came from schools, health staff, lay people, other social services and police or probation. Only 6% were anonymous. The relative frequency of referrals from different sources varied by area.

Less than a third of the children lived with both natural parents. Those referred for neglect or physical abuse were living in more disadvantaged circumstances than those referred for sexual abuse.

for more detailed comparison. During a four month period, all significant referrals were tracked through the system using social services records; those that progressed as far as a case conference were monitored for another 26 weeks.

Wide variations were found between areas in the amount and type of service and the likelihood of de-registration, but it was universally the case that those registered received significantly more in the way of services and that across the different areas the pattern of results was much the same. So, after six months, just over half the children who had been registered were living safely at home, a quarter were at home having experienced further harm and one in five had been removed from home or had left home. In three out of ten cases registered a further incident of abuse or neglect was recorded during the follow-up period.

There was a tendency for authorities who registered fewer children to work in a more selective way and to operate higher thresholds for registration. These operational factors were related to the nature of the local populations and, in particular, to the severity of social deprivation and disorganisation. Low-rate authorities tended to have to deal with lower general levels of social stress and consequently to be better organised and to de-register children more quickly, in the process achieving more rapid turnover. There were also aspects of the working relationship between professional groups that appeared to affect the rate at which different types of maltreatment were recorded.

The researchers found that, once brought to the attention of social services, too many families struggling with child-rearing in difficult circumstances were prematurely defined as potential child protection cases rather than as families in which there were children in need. Front line staff were often compelled to take decisions in a vacuum, unable to refer to any central policy or to apply any proper system of risk assessment. As a result, too many investigations produced neither protective action nor the offer of any other service.

Having admitted a child to the protection system, authorities varied in their ability to collaborate. Inter-agency co-ordination was generally good, but case reviews were not always held within six months of registration and sometimes lacked a sufficiently detailed assessment of continued risk. At the other end of the process, there was wide variation in practice concerning the removal of a child's name from the register. Where the needs of young children at severe risk were concerned, social work practice seemed to be especially good, but the predicament of teenagers who could not remain at home often appeared to have been overlooked.

The important general message was that, while the child protection system came to the rescue of some children in grave danger, large numbers were being drawn in whose needs tended to be neglected as soon as it was established that protective intervention as such was not required. In this study about three quarters of the children 'netted' received no protective intervention and a high proportion received no help of any kind.

Some two-thirds of families were already known to social services departments and 47% had been previously investigated for suspected maltreatment of their children. A substantial minority of parents had histories of criminal behaviour, substance abuse or mental illness. Domestic violence was recorded in over a quarter of cases.

As discouraging was the finding that the better practice observed in some authorities was not reflected in any clear gain in terms of successful results. The conscientious monitoring of the lives of children who remained at home, supplemented with practical help, in other words good service of the standard kind, did not seem to get to grips with the forces that produced maltreatment, nor compensate for its effects on the child. The co-ordination of intervention policies and co-operation between agencies, properly regarded as essential during the process of diagnosis and care planning, were relatively lacking during treatment but were needed just as much.

The evidence concerning case outcome showed that the specialist resources that might make a difference to the development of protected children were largely controlled by the education and health authorities. For there to be further improvement, the emphasis of child protection policy needed to shift towards the development of more specialised training for social workers and the introduction and evaluation of more effective post-case conference services within a collaborative inter-agency framework.

Inter-agency Coordination in Child Protection
Working Together in Child Protection *and*
Coordination and Child Protection: A Review of the Literature
Christine Hallett and Elizabeth Birchall, University of Stirling

These reports contain commentary from six professional groups on the success of inter-agency co-ordination, in particular at child protection case conferences and there is a discussion of each group's perceptions of the contribution and shortcomings of the others. A series of case vignettes is used as a basis for exploring professional attitudes to a range of circumstances commonly encountered in child protection work.

Co-operation in child protection work is mandatory; professionals in any case want to work together because it eases the stress of the task. Nevertheless, organisation theory suggests that co-operation is difficult to achieve. Various studies of professional practice had touched upon the topic but prior to Hallett and Birchall's study there had been no large empirical investigation into the feasibility or value of 'working together' in child protection.

The project was in three parts. The first was a literature review published in 1992. In the second part, the team set about identifying factors that might help or hinder collaboration among professionals. Those asked to take part were general practitioners, health visitors, paediatricians, specialist police, social workers and teachers. All told there were 339 participants, representing a 60% response rate overall, but within that figure there was wide variation between professions, for instance from 81% in the case of health visitors to 38% among general practitioners.

The most striking impression was that the need for co-operation in child protection was every bit as widely recognised as those responsible for policy and guidance would have wished. Most thought the quality of co-operation was good, but only a minority believed the system was working smoothly. So, while there was no sign of severe conflict, there were many frictions and confusions to be reckoned with. The majority who replied had some experience of child protection work, but nearly half had been involved in fewer than ten cases during the previous decade. Again the variation was considerable: some teachers had no experience at all, whereas one senior police child protection co-ordinator could count 2,000 recent cases. Social workers, police and paediatricians emerged as the key figures in the professional network, reflecting the forensic emphasis of the process as it existed. General practitioners and teachers were rarely involved and frequently not well informed, yet, significantly, others who might expect to collaborate with them, had high, if unclear expectations of what both groups had to contribute. The paradox was a good indication of the need for closer attention to the value of professional expertise.

The network was found to operate on four layers. On the first layer were the core professionals such as social workers, paediatricians and the police; on the second the front line agencies, such as schools, health visitors and general practitioners (and, in many cases, social workers, too); on the third, contact professions such as school nurses and education welfare officers, and on the fourth, case-specific professionals, for example lawyers and psychiatrists.

Away from the first level, special training turned out to be very limited, particularly among teachers, general practitioners and junior doctors. Across all groups, half the sample had received no in-service training at all and very few reckoned to have had anything extending to more than a fortnight. For most respondents, some training had involved interdisciplinary work, but generally the inter-professional mix had been narrow. Among those who had been given special training most said they found it useful, but there was less commitment to the benefits of interdisciplinary work than had been hoped. The omission of interdisciplinary training for junior doctors was felt to be particularly regrettable.

As far as collaborative practice was concerned, dealings between social workers and the police seemed remarkably friction-free, particularly by comparison with the testy relationship that existed between many social workers and doctors. The worst examples involved paediatricians: sometimes it seemed that their education and rank blinded them to the expertise and insight of case workers.

Friction to do with tasks or priorities or role confusion within and between the professions was very evident and was responsible for unrealistic or incompatible ideas about what individuals were supposed to do or were capable of doing. And once the cogs of the machine began to grate, it was common for political factors of power and status and resource dependency to intervene and for there to be territorial disputes.

To find out more about how different professionals might respond to different sorts of child protection work, all were asked to rate a series of short vignettes. The exercises showed that profession was the factor that most affected an individual's point of view, not only when fulfilling a task specific to

It emerged that health visitors were most in agreement about the gravity of leaving a child alone in the dark or failing to have an ear infection attended to. Health visitors and teachers were most united in the extent of their concern about the sexualised behaviour of an eight year old girl, whereas social workers were surprisingly divided in their view of that case and of the harmfulness of leaving a child alone after midnight. Curiously, the police were far more outspoken in their horror over a single episode of genital fondling than they were in their response to the case of a small child left to wander on a main road.

There was extremely close consensus within the professional groups regarding vignettes that referred to sexual practices and physical abuse; those that generated least agreement tended to be in the area of neglect, suggesting that neglect was more likely to be overlooked by professionals.

There was little evidence in the case records of repeated, intrusive interviewing of children, and, rather on the contrary, some signs that direct contact with children at the outset might have been rather superficial, resulting in there being too little information for protection conferences about their well-being and reactions to the abuse.

his or her job, but more pervasively, in influencing perceptions of how and by whom any aspect of a case was best dealt with. High levels of consensus were rare and most agreement had much to do with professional posture.

In contrast, variations from place to place in how equivalent professionals regarded policy and the practicalities of collaboration were slight. Local guidelines were very similar, too, so that the researchers were left with the impression of a fairly uniform national culture and a common procedural framework, despite discrepancies between individuals and professions.

Similarly, despite their clear importance in relation to some child protection issues, gender, age and child-rearing experience seemed to have hardly any bearing on the professionals' perceptions concerning the different cases in the questionnaire. Gender, on the other hand, was a factor in some aspects of inter-professional relationships and was intertwined with questions of status. There was evidence, too, that the race of a child affected the perceptions of professionals.

The third part of the study was designed to explore inter-agency policies and practices on two research sites, by evaluating the progress of 48 primary school aged children registered as physically or sexually abused and the degree of co-ordination among the professionals involved.

Beyond the early phase of an investigation, inter-agency co-ordination declined. In almost four cases in ten, social services were the only agency mentioned in the child protection plan and, when others were included, their role was not always made clear. The most prominent form co-ordination took was information exchange, which was abundant at the referral and investigation stages, but less apparent in case intervention, and at reviews. Otherwise there was some joint planning and shared decision making, but not much else.

The profession found at the heart of the inter-agency response to child abuse were the police, who were involved in 32 of the 48 cases and were invited to attend all initial child protection conferences. At the other extreme, general practitioners were the largest group of absentees from initial conferences. They also headed the list of those with roles considered to be 'very' or 'rather' unclear and they were rated by nearly half the respondents as performing 'rather' or 'very' poorly in the child protection context.

Four pillars of inter-agency co-ordination were studied: the child protection register, the child protection conference, local procedural guidelines and the Area Child Protection Committee. The child protection conference and local procedural guidelines were particularly valued. The ACPCs were considered to be performing useful functions but to be hampered by their status, resources and membership. There was a gap to be bridged between the ideal of a Protection Committee as a dynamic grouping of expertise and the frequent reality of a slow and cumbersome creature, lacking teeth and clear vision.

The Extent and Nature of Organised and Ritual Sexual Abuse of Children

by Jean La Fontaine, The London School of Economics

This report includes a comparison of British and American reports, a discussion of the history of witch hunts and the anthropology of witchcraft and description of recent cases. It compares the sociology of ritual and organised abuse and analyses available evidence.

This study was commissioned in the midst of controversy. A number of cases of sexual abuse had been made the more disconcerting by allegations of witchcraft, satanism or devil-worship. There was little hard evidence to support the claims, but the self-confidence of the child protection services was all the same badly affected by the furore that followed. The purpose of Jean La Fontaine's study was to try to establish what had actually taken place in such cases and to decide if there was consequently a new threat to children that had to be reckoned with. The intention was also to consider cases in which ritual was suggested in the context of what was known about the organised sexual abuse of children and to discover the extent and distribution of reported cases.

From a postal survey among police forces, social services departments and the National Society for the Prevention of Cruelty to Children in England and Wales, it emerged that between January 1988 and December 1991, 211 cases of organised abuse had been reported, including 62 where there were allegations of ritual behaviour associated with the abuse. That figure was subsequently increased to 68 after a search was made of case records in eight local authorities, and the total became the basis of the quantitative study.

Permission was also obtained to read all the Official Solicitor's files relating to 34 Wards of Court where there were allegations of ritual abuse. Police and social work files on an additional case reported by the Metropolitan Police and one more (early) case reported by social services were also read, and, from these sources combined, seven representative cases were selected for detailed study. They were chosen to represent the geographical spread of the survey and also the variety of incident described, including one of the very few in which there had been material corroboration that a child had been abused during a ritual. Background material was collected from newspaper reports and other written material and letters describing cases.

Indications of three main types of organised abuse were sought: ritual abuse, paedophile networks and family-based abuse, but they emerged rather as interchangeable strains within a broad band of deviant sexual behaviour. No type was clearly distinguishable and no feature was exclusive to any. Cases were found to be distinguished more by the differing proportion of the characteristics they embodied. So, among paedophile networks there was a preponderance of men abusing boys, whereas organised abuse based on links between and within families, which relied upon a network of relatives, friends and neighbours, involved women and men as perpetrators and boys and girls as victims. Cases where there were allegations of ritual resembled more closely the latter type, but the pattern was not the same in every case: paedophile networks were known to exist where girls were among the victims, and there were cases of family abuse where the victims were all boys. For example, in one case described initially as abuse in a large extended family there was a change in classification some time after the successful prosecution of the main offenders. Three young brothers placed together in a children's home alleged that they had been abused during rituals.

Twenty-three cases of survivors were reported to the study. Most were young women in their twenties although six were older. The fact that many of the cases had come through a therapist indicated the existence of earlier problems and might have accounted for the preponderance of women. Survivors were found to have been very influential. Their stories were said to validate what children said about their experiences, but, at least as significantly, survivors created a climate of belief before any cases involving children were discovered.

No factor could consistently be said to distinguish organised abuse from isolated cases involving a single perpetrator. Perpetrators in organised cases might use different strategies, but the man who befriended a child in order to recruit another victim to a paedophile network was just as likely to behave in the same way as the man who abused neighbourhood children on his own. A man who abused his child might later encourage a friend to participate and then go on to assemble a network of abusers, but, again, there were cases of ritual abuse that showed no sign of development or organisation.

Most cases of organised abuse concerned male perpetrators; in 94 survey cases no women were involved as perpetrators but in only one case was no man involved. Male victims were also frequent, appearing in all but 38 (22%) of the cases and confirming the conclusions of earlier surveys that boys were more vulnerable to abuse outside the home and, according to this survey, to organised abuse. There were no girls in 60 cases (34%).

Another important feature of all such allegations was their rarity. Allegations of ritual were present in only 8% of cases involving organised abuse, which themselves were a very small minority of all child abuse cases. Confirmed cases, in which there was corroborative evidence of ritual, were even rarer: just two emerged during the study period.

Evidence that adults had performed rituals of recognisably occult significance was virtually non-existent; there was even a scarcity of evidence of vaguer interest in the occult. Books about the occult were reported to have been uncovered during three house searches, but in one such instance none of the books contained information about any rituals or offered any justification for the sexual abuse of children that was alleged to have taken place; in the other two cases there was a link, but in only one was it alleged that the ritual followed the prescription in a book. Similarly, during one search, a video of sado-masochistic behaviour was found which was later described as an example of satanic ritual but turned out to have been a recording of performance art; in another case a man and a woman admitted dressing in sheets and pretending to be ghosts to frighten children, but the candles they carried had a more utilitarian purpose: the electricity in the house had been cut off for non-payment.

In all three cases where there was strong evidence that rituals had been held and children sexually abused, what occurred had been contrived by a single central figure who was also the perpetrator of the abuse; in one case no other adult was involved, the others involved one and two more participants respectively. In each case everything mentioned in the victim's statements was found, but none involved any act of killing, whether animal or human, any abortion, bestiality or use of faeces or urine. Thus, it was a significant and paradoxical finding that the ritual whose occurrence was confirmed was quite unlike the ritual described in the uncorroborated allegations. In the confirmed cases a single perpetrator used self-proclaimed spiritual powers to attract children and entrap them; the same 'powers' were used to justify the abuse and intimidate the victims. All the evidence tended to support the view that it was wrong to regard ritual abuse as a phenomenon distinct from sexual abuse. Much of what was alleged to have taken place was merely some known form of sexual deviation; all behaviours were depicted in child pornography.

The most distinctive feature of all the cases was the degree of deprivation out of which they sprang. Nearly three-quarters of the Official Solicitor cases involved very poor people. Many of the men had criminal records, mostly for theft, also for violence. The households were themselves disorganised and violent. The children might all be the offspring of one mother, but hardly ever of a single couple. The children were neglected: they had few clothes, bathed infrequently, had no set times for meals or sleep and possessed few toys. When they were in care they had nightmares. They wet and soiled their beds; they smeared excrement over the walls and themselves; they were found trying to abuse or hurt the pets; they abused younger foster brothers and sisters and their behaviour was often extremely sexualised.

While the children were said over and over again to be exhibiting strange terrors which defied rational explanation, what created an equally strong impression but went unremarked was the fear they induced in the professionals who dealt with them. Many social workers had no knowledge of deviant sexual practices such as sado-masochism, bestiality or the penetration of the anus and vagina with objects. When, in cases like these, they came across behaviour so extreme, particularly in relation to children, they were driven to seek evidence of an event of assault or abuse commensurate with the magnitude of the damage. Some were so deeply shocked that they were prepared to accept the suggestion, to be found in much American fundamentalist writing on the subject, that the acts they heard described were characteristic of satanism and ritualism. In order to reconcile themselves to an intractable abuse case they strayed into the territory of romance – and in the process demonised the marginal poor.

Sexually Abused Children and Adolescents and Young Perpetrators of Sexual Abuse who were Treated in Voluntary Community Facilities

Elizabeth Monck and Michelle New, Institute of Child Health, University of London

This study provides information about sexually abused children and young perpetrators treated in specialist community-based programmes. Background information and psychological data for both groups are considered as well as longitudinal evidence about changes in circumstances and behaviour. It includes similar information about the children's mothers.

This Institute of Child Health study sought to discover the characteristics of sexually abused children, and young perpetrators of sexual abuse, who came to be treated in specialist community-based programmes, as opposed to NHS clinics or programmes run by the probation service.

All cases aged 4 to 18 years who were referred to selected voluntary agency centres were asked to participate, and were included when parents and children agreed. Young perpetrators were included if their sexually offensive behaviour included contact abuse. All victims of sexual abuse were included, whether or not the experience had included physical contact.

Data were collected at three points: at the start of the therapeutic intervention, 12 months later and when treatment ended. At each stage children and parents were asked to fill out self-report questionnaires and parents and teachers completed child behaviour checklists. Therapists were asked to complete schedules concerning demographic information, the nature of the abuse experience or abusive behaviour and the needs of the abused child or young perpetrator. All the responses were sent to the researchers by centre staff.

In a sample of 239 victims, 77% were girls whose average age at referral was 11. Boys were significantly younger than girls at referral. Nearly 80% of the children had been abused by one perpetrator, 93% of whom were males. More than half the perpetrators were fathers (or father figures). Only half the perpetrators had been charged with any offence. Types of abuse were codified into non-contact (19%), contact (52%) and penetrative (31%).

Two-thirds of the victims reported severe depression and a quarter, a significant number of whom had experienced penetrative abuse, said they had thoughts of suicide. Mothers reported high levels of anxiety and depression, and centre workers noted that many needed help with parenting problems or other personal difficulties. Among children neither their depressive mood nor level of self-esteem changed after treatment, but their mothers' self-esteem and parenting skills improved markedly.

All the young perpetrators were boys. Their average age was 15 and half had a previous history of sexual victimisation. Over 80% had abused victims of one gender only, the abusive behaviour extending from touching to rape. The proportion of boys reporting depression was not significantly different from a normal adolescent population, and, clinically, their needs did not suggest severe disturbance in the group as a whole, athough in some cases the problems were pronounced. As with the mothers of victims, the mothers of young perpetrators reported high levels of depression, but only about a quarter were regarded as lacking parenting skills. The number of boys completing questionnaires at the end of the treatment period and after 12 months was small: there appeared to be no significant change in their own scores, or in those of their parents.

Some of the difficulties of collecting reliable and consistent data from the centres suggested that more needed to be done to convince social workers and others of the value of keeping adequate records with regard to case outcome.

Child Sexual Abuse: A Descriptive and Treatment Study

Elizabeth Monck, Elaine Sharland, Arnon Bentovim, Gillian Goodall, Caroline Hyde, and Rebekah Lwin, Institute of Child Health, University of London

This study contains information about the increased recognition of child abuse and its effects, the age of children at the onset and cessation of abuse, types of abuse, children's feelings, parents' reactions to disclosure, the psychological impact of abuse on mother and child, the sexualised behaviour of abused children, their behaviour at school and the childhood experiences of abused children's mothers and carers. The children who entered specialist treatment programmes were assessed again after a year.

As recently as the early 1980s in only about one case in ten did sexually abused children receive any treatment. Among the first to develop a treatment programme was the Hospital for Sick Children in Great Ormond Street, where a team of psychiatrists, social workers and psychologists was assembled under the direction of Arnon Bentovim. Their approach was founded on the principles of family therapy, but it also made use of the pioneering work of Giarretto, an advocate of therapy which brought together parents and children of different ages in otherwise homogeneous groups. Group work was felt to be particularly useful for sexually abused children and adolescents. The Institute study was designed to evaluate the treatment's effectiveness.

The first part of the report describes cases referred to the Department of Psychological Medicine at The Hospital for Sick Children over a period of a year and a half. The second part is an examination of the hypothesis that group therapy may be regarded as a valuable addition to more conventional family work. It also tests ideas about the relationship between the degree, type, severity and duration of abuse, the severity of behavioural and psychological symptoms in abused children, and the importance of the quality of an abused child's relationship with a non-abusing parent.

Included in the descriptive study were 74 families with 99 children aged between four and 15, of whom 78 were girls and 21 were boys. Because of the way families were selected and the Hospital's position as a national centre for referrals, the children's experience of abuse was, on the whole, unusually severe. On average it had lasted for nearly three years, one child in five had been abused by more than one person and more than half the children had experienced penetrative abuse. Biological fathers were the abusers in the largest number of cases, followed by men in the role of father, brothers and other male family or household members. Women had abused children in five cases, but in all except one, men were also involved. Altogether 94 per cent of abusers were male and males were involved in 99 per cent of cases.

Not surprisingly, given the severity of their experiences, the behaviour of many of the children was very disturbed, and they also showed physical symptoms. If mothers were depressed or anxious themselves they tended to be more agitated in their response to an abused child and to hint at more severe behaviour problems. As for the children, one in four described themselves as sad or anxious, betraying a distress that was related to a loss of self-esteem and, so it emerged, to believing that their mothers doubted their accounts of what had befallen them. The behaviour of roughly a quarter of the children was overtly sexualised at the time they were referred to the hospital: among girls this was a measure of relatively severe abuse experienced at a younger age. For children over ten the symptoms of disturbed health and depression were gravest, and among older girls there was a greater tendency to feel somehow personally to blame for what had happened.

The discovery that the children had generally been abused over a longer period than those in equivalent studies when the sample had included cases of abuse by strangers and non-family members, gave rise to a strong intuition that the relationship between perpetrator and victim had a bearing on a child's willingness to make known what had happened. It also seemed to follow that the longer the abuse lasted, the greater was the likelihood of children having endured penetrative abuse and the slimmer the chance that their mothers would readily believe their stories. This unhappy combination of factors began to account for the existence of a small but clinically significant group of particularly disturbed young adolescents.

An attempt was made to isolate 'protective' factors that might in some circumstances limit the damage done by sexual abuse. Three were chosen: the supportive reaction of the mother, carers or non-abusing parents; the mother or carer's belief that abuse had occurred, and positive aspects of a child's relationship with his or her mother or carer. But when the severity of abuse, its duration and the relationship between abuser and abused were taken into account no clear protective effect could be identified. Similarly, direct connections were looked for between the worst cases of penetrative abuse and the

The children were asked to recall what they had felt about the abuse while it was going on. After being encouraged to describe their feelings spontaneously, they were also asked to agree or disagree with one or more adjectives describing the abuse or their feelings. Of the 64 who were interviewed 30 said of their experience that it had been painful, 27 that it was strange, 36 that it was wrong, 34 that it was disgusting, 37 that it was frightening, 10 that it had usually been pleasurable and 8 that they believed it was a normal part of family life. Asked about the effect of abuse 11 said they believed there had been none, two that it had been positive, 21 that it was negative, 15 that they did not know.

The 55 biological mothers were asked to provide some information about their own childhoods. Twelve described their upbringing as providing only poor care and for 10 this also included having no happy memories of their childhood or teens. Even among the majority 42 who felt they had adequate or good care, 16 said they had no happy memories. Thus nearly half, 26, of the women said they had no happy memories of their own childhood.

It had been expected that poor care or unhappy memories would affect the quality of the women's relationships with their own children, but no such effect was identified. Nor was any relationship discernible between the mother's own experience of abuse and her readiness to believe a child's report of abuse.

severest psychological or physical distress but no consistent pattern was found. Children appeared to vary in their reactions to similar experiences. The reason some survived better than others was suggested as a focus for future study.

The families who entered treatment were randomly assigned to receive family work on its own or family work with additional group treatment. The first part of the intervention consisted of meetings every four to six weeks with family members and professionals from the community. Those allocated to group treatment took part in a series of extra meetings, for periods appropriate to the age and role of those taking part. Everyone who received either treatment, particularly the mothers of abused children, showed some sign of improvement, physical or psychological. The children, too, said they felt less depressed and anxious. However, when a comparison was made between those who did and who did not receive the additional group treatment, no significant difference was found on standardised measures.

On the other hand, when the hospital clinicians assessed progress using criteria associated with family therapy, greater impovements were claimed for those who had taken part in group treatment. For example, it was said that children were able to share their pain with others and that adult carers were able to agree on what damage had been done. Mothers were also rated by the clinicians as having made better progress.

A possible explanation for this difference of scientific opinion was that group work might well have been shown to deepen, for example, a girl's understanding of who bore the responsibility for the abuse she had suffered, but that a higher degree of comprehension might not make her any less depressed. The research team suggested that changes in attitude might lead to an improvement in psychiatric state and self-esteem over periods longer than the study could investigate.

The team were able to extract several less equivocal messages from their research: first, there was clear evidence that a treatment programme (with or without group work) conducted over a period of about a year could reduce depression and anxiety and improve the self-esteem of the mothers of sexually abused children. By the same route mothers reported fewer behaviour problems in their children and some aspects of the relationship between them also improved. As far as the children were concerned it seemed likely that no major change in self-reported depression or self-esteem could be expected during the first year of treatment, but that was not to deny that significant changes in family dynamics might have been set in train which could lead to a significant improvement later.

What emerged as forcibly was a need for those involved with sexually abused children to pay more careful attention to how the work they undertook might best be evaluated. Above all, there were questions of definition: it was vital that the assessment of children before and after treatment should be standardised and that there should be agreement about what was meant by success, whether for individual cases or for treatment programmes.

Professional Intervention in Child Sexual Abuse

Elaine Sharland, David Jones, Jane Aldgate, Hilary Seal and Margaret Croucher, University of Oxford

This report contains information about the characteristics of cases and interventions, the impact on parents and children of the first investigation, including extracts from interviews, an examination of professional services and an analysis of case outcomes. There is a discussion of the relationship between interventions and of the implications for policy and practice of the findings.

Several social workers had qualms about adhering to policies and procedures which, though well intentioned, seemed to ignore the needs of the child. They were concerned, for instance, that the 'fresh pair of eyes' policy which dictated that someone other than the caseworker interview the child in an open case, could, if applied too rigidly, deny the child the support of a known social worker. The policy could be differently applied even in the same team. Thus in one case a recently qualified social worker was not allowed to support any of the family members and was completely marginalised by the investigating team, whereas an experienced worker in another case was able to maintain a supportive involvement throughout the investigation.

It was a concern at the time the studies were commissioned that the process of investigating sexual abuse cases might be capable of doing harm over and above that caused by the abuse itself. With that anxiety in mind and to remedy what was in any event a scarcity of hard evidence on how well the protection system was operating, the Oxford University group considered what happened when suspicions of sexual abuse were brought to professional attention.

Based on an examination of consecutive referrals over a nine month period in Oxfordshire, their work describes how the intervention was regarded by children, parents and professionals and attempts to analyse the relationship between the style and tone of an enquiry and how successfully cases turned out.

The team collected data from 147 families, including information about how suspicions had been referred, how allegations had been disclosed and the type of intervention which the children and parents had experienced. There was also a more intensive study concerning 41 children who had undergone at least one investigative interview. In those cases the children themselves and their parents or main carers were interviewed and asked to complete questionnaires.

At the outset, the parents' response to an abuse allegation was commonly one of shock, guilt and a profound sense of loss. The release of mixed emotions was frequently misinterpreted or underestimated by social workers so that, for instance, a mother might be described as resigned when in fact she was numb with distress or be referred to as 'over the top' when she was dealing with an eruption of painful memories. Similarly, the sheer variety of the cases in terms of the ages of children and potential perpetrators of abuse, whether they concerned families previously known to social services, the type of abuse suspected, whether it was believed to have occurred inside or outside the family — all these factors combined to put great stress upon the system. In such trying circumstances, the validity of professional judgements and the capacity of the agency network to make support and wise counsel available had to be questionable.

As the study progressed, the team came increasingly to doubt whether protection procedures were always adequate to deal with sexual abuse referrals, because the cross currents of general need and specific risk uncovered by an investigation were often very complex, and sometimes it was impossible to distinguish one from the other. In a sample where nearly half the cases were found not to have involved sexual abuse, it was notable that the less specific needs of families were such that they started to receive social work support soon after the investigation was concluded. However, it emerged that support was more readily available to some families than others, depending on their circumstances, and, rather alarmingly, that those affected by abuse that had occurred outside the close family received least help. Therapeutic interventions for families and children were even rarer and more likely still to be limited to cases where the abuser was a member of the close family.

It appeared on the whole that services were reaching those who needed them and that more follow-through services were made available in cases where the certainty that a child had been abused was most complete. On the other hand, no direct connection was found between the amount of support families received and what parents said they needed, nor were the needs and wishes which parents declared linked to the conclusiveness of the evidence that a child had been abused, to the gravity of the case or to the whereabouts of the perpetrator. The impression that fairly random forces were at work was similar when the researchers considered the consistency and continuity of service provision. They found that although many families had not welcomed the professional intrusion into their lives at first, they had benefited from it and recognised its value; the trouble was that later, when they would have welcomed continuing support with more open arms, none was forthcoming and they felt abandoned. The lack of follow-through service once the initial intervention had occurred had a marked impact on the well-being of children and parents. There was a clear lack of comprehensive assessment and casework, as well as psychological or psychiatric treatment.

When the first round of interviews was conducted, over half the children were considered safe from abuse, and a quarter generally unsafe. Another fifth (19%) were felt not to be safe even from the alleged perpetrator because blank denial by parents that any abuse had occurred was a feature of the case. Nine months later the picture had not changed much. Of 37 children, six were still thought to be unsafe even from the original abuser and 10 more were considered unsafe generally. An unexpectedly strong link emerged between this safety rating and a child's degree of depression, especially in the longer term, but there was no relationship between how depressed children were considered to be by the researchers and how safe *they* felt themselves to be. Thus it seemed that many children in the sample were at risk for reasons over and above that for which they were referred.

The mental health of children showed only limited improvement, and for a significant minority, likely also to be in the unsafe group at follow-up, it deteriorated. Parents' mental health was better at the one year point, but the improvement had no obvious cause: it did not appear to be related to their view of the helpfulness of the intervention or to their ability to establish a workable relationship with professionals. For many it seemed, the abuse allegation was just another affliction to be endured in a generally stressful life.

An acceptable level of partnership between parents and professionals was felt to have been established in just under half the cases. Wherever good relationships were encountered, the key elements generally had more to do with professional style than any particular action, so that parents who felt they were being listened to and, where possible, involved in the investigative process, were most likely to have positive feelings about the process. The same degree of compatibility and consensus was more difficult to achieve where families were already known to social services.

In one particularly unfortunate case of joint working, the child in question was five years old and had been removed from school without her mother's knowledge. The social worker felt powerless to intervene, for fear of making the situation even worse.
'She was away from familiar surroundings. There were no prior meetings. We were unknown people. It was a disruption of her normal day. She was presented with direct questions and made aware her behaviour worried others, which could have induced enormous guilt in her. She was made to continue longer than she wished. She asked to go and play and hid behind the sofa. She was kept in the room against her will, I believe. She was totally bewildered and made anxious by it.'

Some parents simply did not seem to be able to make the connection between the difficulties they experienced and the possibility of professional support or to imagine that agencies which had entered their lives as investigators might also offer a supportive or therapeutic service. One parent, well aware that she and her daughter needed help, had been offered therapeutic support, but had little conception of what that might be. When none materialised she was confused enough to wonder whether a brief doorstep visit by a social work team manager had been 'the treatment'.

Disappointment in the relationship was most severe where there was a failure to bring criminal prosecutions of known and confirmed abusers, and most striking among the cases were those of three parents, who, despite being denied the vindication of a prosecution, managed to offer their children sustained responsiveness and protection. The researchers found them among the most heart-rending in their accounts of their disappointment at the failure to bring their daughters' abusers to trial. The depths of the disservice done to them and its impact on them and their children was not to be underestimated.

There was persuasive evidence that the style of professional behaviour in the early stages of an investigation did have an effect on case outcome, and that the establishment of a working partnership between primary carers and professionals, focusing on the needs and welfare of the child, was an important sign that the intervention had served its purpose. Thus the findings drew attention to the importance of skills training, continuing education and supervision of front line workers and, by implication, to the need to consider whether the social worker responsible for the first part of an investigation was always best placed to undertake vital pastoral work in the longer term.

Evidence of persistent unmet need, deficient follow-through casework and an absence of adequate treatment and counselling services pointed to a need to improve services generally and to redress the balance between child protection on one side and child welfare on the other.

Normal Family Sexuality and Sexual Knowledge in Children

Marjorie Smith and Margaret Grocke, Department of Child Psychiatry, Institute of Child Health, University of London

This study provides information on children's sexual knowledge and exposure to explicit situations in ordinary families. The problems of defining abuse are considered in the light of this evidence.

Most child abuse research has focused on 'abnormal' sexual development and sexual pathologies of childhood to the extent that more is known about sexual deviance than normality or ordinariness. Over-sexualised behaviour is one of the frequently reported consequences of sexual abuse, but the lack of knowledge about normal sexual behaviour and cognition makes it difficult to make judgements about the degree or likely causes of any abnormality.

This study examined parental behaviour and attitudes on sexual matters and linked them to children's concepts and sexual thinking, in order to provide a baseline from which to view the deviant attitudes or behaviour in sexually abusing families. Information was collected about children's sexual knowledge, about sexual behaviour in normal children and family behaviour, and attitudes to sexuality and sexual matters.

It was hypothesised that a child's sexual knowledge would be related to age, and to other factors such as whether he or she had a sibling of the opposite sex and whether there was discussion of sexual topics within the family, and that a wide range of 'normal' family behaviours would be documented.

Although maltreatment can occur in a variety of settings, the evidence on normal behviour is important in defining what is abnormal or abusive. But this approach is problematic. What might be thought of as 'normal' in one generation or social context is often viewed as 'abnormal' in another. Nevertheless, by examining what typically happens in families, this study sheds light on the way abuse comes to be defined.

The sample comprised two groups: children aged between four and 15.11 years randomly selected from general practitioners' lists (the community group), and a smaller group in the same age range, who had attended a hospital clinic with a diagnosis of sexual abuse. For purposes of statistical analyses children in the latter group were matched by sex, social class and, where possible, family size with children in the former. In the study of the community group 172 families were contacted, 146 of whom agreed to participate and were included in the study. Qualifying families had no known history of child abuse; the child had no major physical or mental handicap and the mother spoke English well enough to be interviewed.

Information was collected from semi-structured interviews with mothers or primary carers and from open, child-led interviews with the children. The mothers' interview covered aspects of family behaviour and their observations about their children's sexual knowledge. The child interview explored hobbies, activities, and family and social relationships as well as sexual knowledge. Other information was gathered using self-esteem measures, ambiguous pictures and pictures of naked bodies to elicit sexual knowledge.

Most children had behaved in ways that could be classified as sexual at some time: 63% had touched their mother's breasts and 70% had come into their parents' bed at least weekly. Sixty-six per cent had been seen masturbating and 75% claimed to have seen sexual intimacy on television. The figures for more explicit material, however, were lower; 12% had touched their parents' genitalia, 2% had certainly witnessed sexual intercourse, 18% had definitely seen violent or horror movies and 7% pornographic magazines.

The results indicated a wide variation in sexual knowledge across children's age groups and a wide range of behaviours in families. Family practices and behaviours changed as children grew older. For example, the proportion of children seeing their parents naked decreased with age, from 72% for four to seven year olds to 33% for 12 to 16 year olds. Similarly, bathing with parents was reported for 60% of children but decreased well before puberty. Children often initiated change themselves as they became more modest. There was a tendency for behaviours to be linked. Parents who bathed with their children were more likely to report genital touching. Mothers who were more accepting of a child's masturbation were more likely to have observed it. This may also have reflected a reporting factor, in that parents who were willing to report one behaviour found it easier to report others.

There were consistent and pervasive differences in the results and in child-rearing attitudes according to social class, and, to a lesser extent, gender. Although there was still a wide range within categories, manual social class families tended to be more restrictive in their practices and attitudes. For example, they reported less nudity in their families and less discussion of sexual matters within the household.

Girls had more detailed knowledge about their own sex, for example, in their description of physical changes at puberty, and there was a suggestion that they were able to provide a more detailed description than boys of male changes at puberty. Mothers discussed sexual matters in more detail with their daughters, so increasing their knowledge and vocabulary.

Excessive masturbation, over-sexualised behaviour, an extensive sexual curiosity or sexual knowledge and genital touching are thought to be indicators of sexual abuse. But since these behaviours were found to be common within a community sample, they were not in themselves sufficient to suggest abuse. Family nudity was a pointer to other sexual behaviours within the families. It was also clear that a small but significant number of children who had not been abused, had been in situations or had access to sources which could have given them explicit sexual knowledge.

Parental Control within the Family: The Nature and Extent of Parental Violence to Children

Marjorie Smith, Penney Bee, Andrea Heverin and Gavin Nobes, Thomas Coram Research Unit, University of London

This study contains information about patterns of parental control in a community population. It reports on punishment, discipline and control strategies used by parents, and on the nature of parental authority over children. Data are provided on two minority ethnic groups as well as on the indigenous population.

Normal behaviour in a culture is a major predeterminant of what is defined as abusive. However, a survey of family violence in the United States by Straus, Gelles and Steinmetz reported levels of domestic violence much higher than would have been predicted from available knowledge of child maltreatment. They found that three-quarters (73%) of parents had used some form of violence on their children, and that three-fifths (63%) had done so in the previous year. Violence was defined broadly and most commonly included spanking or slaps (58%) or pushing or shoving (41%). More severe punishment was uncommon, yet nearly one in ten children (8%) had been kicked, beaten or punched, and 3% had been threatened by their parents with a knife or a gun at some time in their lives. Until the work of the Thomas Coram Research Unit was complete, no comparable findings on the extent of domestic violence to children in Britain were available. The best information came from the Newsons' longitudinal study of child rearing practices in 700 families living in Nottingham in the 1960s and 70s.

Mothers were interviewed on a range of topics, including general discipline and punishments, when their children were aged one, four, seven, eleven and sixteen. The majority of mothers reported smacking their children and most thought it right to do so. By four years of age, 97% of children had been smacked and 83% of mothers believed in smacking. (These data provide abuse enquiries with a valuable context, but they do not form a complete picture, since any study of parenting is unlikely to extend to violent behaviour commonly thought to be abusive.)

The Thomas Coram team focused on 403 families drawn at random from the total population in two geographical areas. Each family selected had a child in one of the four age groups; one, four, seven or eleven years. Area One was a town with a population of 60,000, 30 miles from central London. Area Two, within inner London, was less prosperous and had relatively high rates of unemployment, public housing and lone parent families.

The researchers interviewed the 403 mothers, nearly one in four (99) of the fathers and 215 of the children. In addition to demographic information, interviews covered three main areas: the nature and extent of punishment to children (family punishment and control practices, attitudes and beliefs on discipline), factors which may be associated with high levels of physical punishment (such as parental mental health, marital status, or family violence), and the parent/child relationship and child behaviour. Parents were also asked to complete standardised behaviour ratings on their child, which were supplemented by a teacher rating of the children's behaviour and, of course, information from the children themselves.

Control strategies were categorised into three groups: physical, non-physical and non-punitive. The approach was to treat each as part of a continuum, from more 'ordinary' and mild parenting behaviours to less ordinary and more extreme examples of the same behaviour. Information was obtained on the nature of the action involved in physical punishment (what is described as a smack may vary from a tap on the arm to a severe beating) and the context in which it occurred. Parents were asked if they ever smacked or hit their children and also about punishment by example (things such as pinching the child, or hair-pulling), physical restraint and shaking and ingestion (ranging from making a child finish off unwanted food, to forced ingestion of noxious substances). Non-physical control strategies considered included withdrawing things the child liked, such as television or sweets, excluding children, for example by sending them to their room, reparation or fining, or emotional blackmail. Non-punitive control strategies relied on reasoning, distraction, praise, incentives and rewards.

Smacking was the commonest form of punishment, in terms of the number of children who had experienced it. Nine out of every ten surveyed had been hit. Three-quarters of the one year olds had been smacked in the year preceding the interview, as had almost all of the four year olds and seven year olds and half of the eleven year olds. Most children were hit on the hand or the clothed bottom. Very few parents had ever marked their child as a result of hitting them but nearly half of the mothers interviewed were definite that they had smacked their children hard enough to hurt. Most smacking was an irritated or angry response rather than a controlled one. The severity of physical control was assessed, taking into account the intention or potential to cause harm or the use of implements. Most children received mild punishment but 15% had experiences which could be categorised as severe. Some forms of punishment, such as biting or punching, or forcing children to eat, were rare, but were still reported by some parents.

Some other forms of control were commonly experienced by children. Nearly three-quarters of mothers had excluded their children as a form of

Mothers considered themselves to be the principal punishers in their family, a view not always shared by fathers who often saw themselves as taking a punitive stance. In fact, mothers were more likely to hit their children than fathers. This difference was not only a consequence of fathers spending less time with their children. Even when care of the offspring was equally shared, fathers hit less.

The researchers read children short vignettes of different situations in which a child was being naughty: in one the child was being disobedient, in another fighting with a brother or sister; in a third doing something dangerous; and in the last stealing money. The worse the behaviour, the more severe was the punishment suggested by the children. About a quarter of children proposed a physical punishment for each of the vignettes, and the boys were more punitive than the girls. Overall, just over half the children thought it was right for their parents to smack them and most said they intended to smack their offspring.

punishment and a half had stopped their children doing something that they wanted (most often this was not letting them watch television or go out with friends). These forms of control were increasingly used with older children; and hitting became less common with age. Most punishment was used by parents who were generally warm and supportive. Rewards and praise of children were frequent; at least half of children were praised daily.

Just under half the mothers interviewed felt that children did not misbehave deliberately. Another third saw misbehaviour as limit-testing by children seeing how far they could go; it was deliberate but not malicious. Three-quarters of mothers and an even greater proportion of fathers thought that there should not be any laws against smacking in the home. However, three-fifths of mothers thought that teachers should not be allowed to use physical punishment in schools.

The researchers found a wide range of normal parenting styles. Family relationship variables, such as the quality of the marital relationship, family violence, and the amount of aggression between siblings, were more strongly predictive of high levels of physical punishment, than were demographic indicators such as marital status, social class, or poor housing. The team concluded that the context in which control was exerted on children was important. Three per cent lived in situations low in warmth and a similar proportion in households high in criticism. It was in these environments that repeated physical punishment was likely to be harmful.

Paternalism or Partnership? Family Involvement in the Child Protection Process
June Thoburn, Ann Lewis and David Shemmings, University of East Anglia

This study includes a discussion of the background to the concept of working in partnership and contains a detailed account of social work in 220 cases. Case study material includes interviews with parents, children and relatives. The nature and extent of family involvement and the characteristics of working in partnership are described. There is an analysis of 33 child protection conferences.

The research studies were commissioned by the Department of Health before *Working Together* was revised in 1991 but after the *Children Act* 1989 had made it clear that agencies should aim to work in partnership with families in all child care cases. At the time, practice across the country varied, especially where family involvement in child protection conferences was concerned, and there was uncertainty about whether notions of partnership were always practicable or even desirable. The East Anglia study set out to examine the issues of participation from several points of view.

Working in three London boroughs, a northern district, one county in the Midlands and two in the South East, the team wanted to discover the extent to which family members were involved in routine child protection work and whether attempts to work in partnership appeared to be to the benefit or detriment of children or parents. Their study describes how agencies and workers sought to involve family members in protection, support and the therapeutic processes and considered links between the degree of involvement achieved and the characteristics of the families, the type of abuse and agency and social work practice.

During 1990 and 1991 the progress of 220 consecutive child protection cases was closely followed by means of file searches and interviews with social workers, parents, and some children and relatives. In their general complexion the cases were similar to those considered at case conferences in the country as a whole, except that family members were more likely to be present because the social work teams selected had declared an intention to work in partnership with them. A sub-sample of 33 cases was identified for more detailed study, the main criterion being that the parents should be willing to take part in the research.

Information about whether there was agreement on the nature of and responsibility for the abuse was combined with an assessment of the stresses inside the families to produce a researcher's rating of the obstacles to working in partnership. As time went by, note was also taken of the methods agencies and workers used to encourage family members to be involved, and of how parents and children reacted. At the six month stage a further rating was given of the degree of participation in the case and of how well the case was progressing.

Parents or carers were asked if they felt they had been kept informed, if they understood what had been happening in the course of child protection procedures, if they contributed to the plans and felt they had taken part in the decision making. Fifty seven per cent said they understood, 43 per cent said they contributed, but only 35 per cent said they took part in the decision making. At a general level, just over half said they felt they had been involved in the proceedings, just under half said they had not.

Case outcome was considered to be good if various general criteria could be said to have been met. Note was taken of whether a child's living and parenting arrangements appeared to be settled, whether he or she was living with or in contact with parents and other adults held dear, whether there was evidence of emotional and developmental progress and whether professional support was a match for the problems that had been identified. Using these considerations as a basis, the researchers found a clear link between better outcomes for children and greater involvement of parents. Parents were involved in 53 per cent of cases where the outcome was good, 24 per cent in which it was considered poor.

A failure to work in partnership could often be attributed to aspects of a particular case, but, significantly, the differences between cases where family members were well-informed and fully consulted and cases where communication was poor could almost always be traced to aspects of agency procedures. There was no evidence that things ever turned out badly for children or parents as a result of working in partnership.

To a degree, the likelihood of involvement bore a direct relation to the sort of problems that existed in a family. Nevertheless, in only 22% of cases in the

Where the allegation was sexual abuse or over-chastisement teenage girls were most likely to be in the poor outcome group. Cases were more likely to be in the good outcome group when parents with whom the children continued to live were not implicated in the mistreatment.

The term 'emotional abuse' was found by some parents to be particularly unhelpful and inappropriate to the position as they saw it. In discussions with them and in considering their cases it appeared that emotional neglect was a better phrase. There were some cases in which emotional abuse had occurred in that they involved elements of deliberate cruelty and desire to harm, but even in some of those the term was unhelpful because the parent was suffering from a mental illness or personality disorder and was powerless to do much about his or her behaviour.

An early observation was the need parents had for written as well as verbal information about all stages in the child protection process. The questions parents most commonly needed written answers to were:

Will my child be taken away from me?

My child has been taken away how do I get him/her back?

What is my legal position?

How do I find out what is going on?

What am I being accused of?

Are you labelling me?

What is the register and who gets put on it?

What is a case conference?

Can I go to the conference?

Can I be given written informa-tion?

Who will help me in all this?

What should I do next?

Is there anyone else to turn to apart from social services?

I want to complain, how do I do it?

'best scenario' group, those for whom a partnership was considered eminently possible, was anything quite as constructive achieved. At the other end of the scale, 9% of those ascribed by researchers to the 'worst scenario' group in terms of the likelihood of becoming involved, were rated as participating in the social work to an acceptable degree.

The number of cases in which the problems of parents and children were so severe that it proved not to be possible to involve them at all turned out to be very small, and, even in circumstances when the degree of difficulty meant that a poor outcome was almost inevitable, some workers did manage to secure some semblance of participation in the process. Where a high degree of participation was achieved in the face of clear obstacles, the key factors were the attitudes, skill and efforts of social workers who were in turn able to rely on agency policies and procedures which encouraged them to be creative in their thinking.

All family members stressed the importance of being cared about as people. They could understand that the professional had a job to do and that proce-dures were necessary, but they strongly objected to workers in whatever profession who did not appear to listen, did not show warmth or concern or who did things only by the book. Among parents, both those who were implicated in the abuse of their children and those who were not, these basic opinions about what mattered were the same.

Children expressed very similar opinions about the process to those of their parents, but most objected strongly to being interviewed at school, especially whenever they were taken out of classes for the purpose. On the few occasions when young people attended case conferences they were almost invariably unprepared and it was obvious that much more needed to be done to help them participate. And, since the main point at issue at a case confer-ence concerned the behaviour of parents, it was considered questionable whether the distress sometimes caused to children watching from the sidelines of an adult world was justified. Doubt was greatest when the behaviour of parents whose children were living with them at home was being anatomised.

Clear, too, was the need for those who chaired conferences to demonstrate that they were not prepared merely to rubber stamp strategies assembled elsewhere. The most common complaint the team heard was 'They'd made up their minds before we came in.' There was evidence to support that view: important contributions sometimes went unheeded just because they did not sit easily with the opinions conference members brought with them.

Another danger was that apparent agreement at a multi-disciplinary con-ference might disguise a lack of family members' participation in other aspects of case management. There were occasions, especially if children were looked after, when it seemed that parents and workers lurched from one set piece to the next, between times never seeing each other except on the eve of another conference, when parents were showered with the drafts of the latest case reports.

Related studies

An Exploratory Study of the Prevalence of Sexual Abuse in a Sample of 16-21 Year-Olds

Liz Kelly, Linda Regan and Sheila Burton, University of North London

The report includes comparisons between the experiences of white, Asian and African Caribbean respondents and the prevalence of multiple abuse among disabled and non-disabled respondents. There is information about the relationship between abuser and abused according to the type of experience and about the consequences of incidents in terms of disclosure and long-term effect.

In previous prevalence studies of child sexual abuse in Britain and America there were wide discrepancies in the scale of the problem considered to have been uncovered. Different methodologies and choices of definition had given dramatically different results, to the extent that estimates of the proportion in the general population who had been sexually abused varied from one in ten to one in two.

This retrospective study of abuse experienced in childhood by a group of British college students sought to provide more accurate data by constructing a methodology that took better account of variations in definition and the influence of factors to do with gender, ethnicity and disability.

Colleges of further education were used as the focus of the survey because they assembled students of varying abilities on a wide range of vocational, technical and academic courses. Young people could be approached away from their home environment and so free of any parental pressure, although the same strategy meant that certain significant groups, such as prostitutes and runaways, were excluded. Another drawback, as it turned out, was an imbalance between the sexes: 62% of the sample were women.

To unravel the problems associated with the definition of abuse, a spectrum of behaviour was inquired into including indecent exposure, unwanted touching, coerced sex and rape. Also included were incidents of attempted abuse and strategies associated with successful resistance.

It emerged that, by the broadest definition, 59% of women and 27% of men reported at least one experience of sexual abuse. If sexual abuse was defined as any unwanted sexual event or interaction, then over one woman in two and one man in four had had such an experience before they were 18.

Most common reported forms of experience were flashing and touching; when these were excluded from the reckoning, the incidence lessened to one woman in five and one man in 14. The more serious incidents such as forced sex, rape or coerced masturbation were experienced by one women in 25 and one man in 50. Both men and women said that their chief reason for confiding in someone had been to gain corroborative support. Reasons for silence were more complicated: women pointed to the fear of being disbelieved, men tended to be silent out of feelings of guilt or shame. In all, only 2% of the people studied had been to any official support agency, so highlighting the need for informal but skilled support networks.

The questionnaire was formulated by the researchers and modified during a trial with students at two polytechnics. Its principal refinement was the multiple probe, by which questions of a similar nature were repeated at different points in modified contexts. Offering multiple probes had been found to increase the reporting of incidents of abuse by jogging the memory giving reassurance and encouraging participants to reveal an experience they had initially decided not to reveal.

Differences in the way men and women described the long-term effects of abuse gave the impression that women are more aware than men of their own vulnerability. Men were less inclined than women to associate memories of incidents with feelings of fear and pain, but in their coping strategies both sexes considered trying to forget or to minimise its significance to be the best way forward.

Prevalence of forms of sexual abuse for the whole sample and by gender	All %	Women %	Men %
Flashing	19	25	8
Touching	17	21	10
Unwanted attempts	16	20	8
Pressurised sex	12	16	5
Rape	4	5	2
Ambivalent response	3	4	2
Forced masturbation	3	4	1
Pornography	0	0	0

When research gives incidence rates based only on reported cases of sexual abuse, family members tend to be over-represented statistically. Incest was shown to be relatively uncommon, but to achieve prominence because of its emotional and psychological ramifications. At another extreme, the researchers considered that there was a tendency to overlook the fact that in other settings, for example in residential homes, ample opportunities existed for repeated abuse.

The study sought to establish whether certain groups were more vulnerable to being the victims of multiple assaults. People with disabilities seemed to be at particular risk, but the numbers in this study were not large enough to be thought significant.

A question little addressed by earlier research which came to prominence during the study was the extent and significance of sexual abuse by peers. The abuse of children by other children tended to be dismissed as innocent experimentation or as a manifestation of acting out behaviour by children who had been abused themselves, but neither view addressed the problem of the unabused child who abused others. In adolescence the problem was taken more seriously, as studies of 'date rape' showed, but the underlying question of whether peer abuse was to be treated as a distinct phenomenon had received less attention.

Little evidence emerged of abuse by women, but it was considered to be another important issue because opinion had become so polarised between those who regarded it as extremely traumatic and those who regarded it as relatively unimportant. In this study there was evidence to indicate that men abused by women regarded the experience as quite positive, perhaps because they reconstructed what had happened in their own minds and in the process imputed to themselves a more 'masculine' measure of control.

Men and women were divided on the subject of punishment of abusers: women spoke of the need for treatment, men tended to advocate severe punishment.

Child Sexual Abuse in Northern Ireland: A Research Study of Incidence
The Research Team, Queen's University, Belfast

This study calculates the rate of child sexual abuse in Northern Ireland. It discusses problems of definition, measurement, interpretation and makes comparisons with data from other countries.

This study sought to establish the number of new sexual abuse cases occurring in Northern Ireland during 1987, at a time when incidence studies of child abuse were rare and the use of strict epidemiological definitions rarer. Such an approach was valuable, it was argued, because the data could easily be combined with published population figures to produce estimates of risk to children in the community according to their age and sex, and by studying the pattern over several years it would become possible to find out how the problem was evolving and so to plan and co-ordinate specialist services.

More than 28 professional and statutory agencies co-operated, including social services, police, probation, the forensic medical service, child psychiatrists, general practitioners and the NSPCC. During the study period 946

A broad, clear, practical and easily interpreted definition was required in order to identify all potential cases of child sexual abuse, and so the following, based on Baker and Duncan, was adopted and printed on the notification form: 'A child, anyone under 17 years, is sexually abused when one or more persons involves the child in any activity for the purpose of their own sexual arousal. This might involve intercourse, touching, exposure of sexual organs, showing porno-graphic material, or talking about sexual things in an erotic way etc.' It differed from Baker and Duncan's by incorporating the age of consent for girls in Northern Ireland (17, not 16 years), and by allowing for the possibility that a child might be abused by more than one person. It also allowed for sibling incest and peer group sexual activity.

incident notifications were received. After duplicates, false allegations and cases for which there was too little information had been excluded, the remaining 870 cases relating to 598 children were analysed. The cases of 416 children had been notified once, the remainder more than once by different reporters. The principal sources of the information were police (32%), social workers (21%) and forensic medical officers (16%).

From the outset it was recognised that the number of cases brought to light at each level of the process of assessment would depend greatly on how child sexual abuse was defined. The definition the researchers devised was designed to pick up all types of sexual abuse; nevertheless, among the returns from reporters only 33 (6%) could be classified as non-contact abuse. Of the 598 children, half experienced penetrative abuse and another third (31%) experi-enced non-penetrative sexual abuse.

The incidence rate for all types of abuse reported was 1.3 per 1,000, but that figure was first modified on the basis that only 408 of the 598 could be regarded as established cases and that there was consequently a danger of making an overestimate. Taking the established cases, the rate was thus reduced to 0.9 per 1,000 children. Among those represented in the established cases, 94% had experienced physical sexual abuse.

For boys and girls the incidence rates were 0.34 and 1.49, indicating a risk ratio of 4.4 girls to every boy. Among children aged 0-4 years the rate was relatively low, 0.28 cases per 1,000, but it rose steadily across the age range to 1.91 cases per 1,000 among children in the oldest age group (15-16 years). Among boys, the age pattern was significantly different from that observed in girls and peaked at 0.5 cases per 1,000 in the 5-9 year age group. For girls the rate increased with age to a maximum of 3.73 cases per 1,000 among those aged 15-16 years, but in that age group, 22 had been abused by boyfriends in circumstances where there was evidence of consent. When these data were eliminated the incidence rate for the group fell from 3.73 to 2.92.

The simplest definition of incidence ignored the possibility that suspected or alleged cases might eventually become established, and on that basis there were grounds for saying that it was too conservative. Consequently, suspected and alleged cases were re-examined and 119 were identified whose character-istics were indistinguishable from the 408 cases in the established group. Revising the calculations raised the incidence rate by 29% from 0.9 to 1.16 cases per 1,000. An attempt was made to extrapolate the findings. The table below shows estimates of annual incidence for Scotland, England and Wales based on the Northern Ireland figures.

Region	Observed	Predicted	Adjusted [a]	
Northern Ireland	408	527	846	*[a] On the basis of an ascer-tainment rate of 62%*
Scotland	1,017	1,311	2,114	
England and Wales	9,823	12,661	20,411	
UK total	11,248	14,499	23,371	

The rate for Northern Ireland was found to be higher than any reported from elsewhere in the UK, but marginally lower than the rates of 2.2 and 2.5 indicated by Finkelhor and Hotaling from a national study in the USA. The lowest estimate of 0.9 established cases per 1,000 children was 5.3 times higher than the rate reported in 1983 by Mrazek et *al.* and 1.6 times the 1986 figure for England and Wales given by the NSPCC, but the latter estimates were derived from 'at risk' registers, which, because of the way they were compiled and the primary purpose they were meant to serve, were known to underestimate incidence. Significantly, in Northern Ireland in 1987 the total recorded on such registers by the four health boards as having been sexually abused was 185 – fewer than half the number of established cases reported to the study.

Predicting the regional incidence of child sexual abuse in the absence of nationally agreed population-based rates proved difficult. The researchers commented that their estimates provided only a first approximation to regional incidence. The figures might be useful for monitoring and for comparative purposes, but generally the actual number of new cases observed in an area would depend on a variety of factors, including the true incidence rate, the population at risk, the definition of child sexual abuse employed and methods of reporting and ascertainment, as well as other social, legal, and cultural factors.

Evaluating Parenting in Child Physical Abuse

Lorraine Waterhouse, Tom Pitcairn, Janice McGhee, Jenny Secker and Cathleen Sullivan, the University of Edinburgh

This study considers the characteristics of children and families involved in cases of physical abuse. It interprets specific incidents in the context of the relations between parents and children, particularly issues of control.

This Economic and Social Research Council study took as a random sample 43 consecutive physical abuse cases referred to three social work departments in Scotland and attempted to analyse the quality of the day-to-day interaction between the children and their parents.

First hand accounts of the parents' routine child-rearing practice were collected and compared with similar assessments made by the social workers involved in the early stages of an investigation. Parents also completed standard questionnaires designed to assess behavioural disturbance in children and to identify any with neurotic or antisocial disorders. To extend the comparison, social workers completed similar questionnaires.

The ordinariness of the study sample was considered important, because it meant that, in terms of the range of their experience, the families could be said to be typical of those in which children were perceived to be at risk of harm and professionals thought fit to intervene. Thus, some parents denied the accusation entirely and some children showed no clear evidence of abuse.

The majority of the parents grew up in Scotland and came from united families. One in three mothers and one in four fathers spent part of their childhood in public care, usually a children's home. None described abuse in

Contact with the law in childhood and in adulthood was a striking feature in the biographies of the parents, especially fathers, half of whom had appeared at a juvenile court or children's hearing, compared with 30 per cent of mothers. Overall, eight out of ten fathers had been in trouble with the law by the time of the research interview, with 50 per cent going to prison or borstal or both. None of these offences was child related. The pattern was much less marked for the mothers.

childhood as a factor in their admission to care, but about a third recalled having had out of the ordinary health or behavioural problems and a significant proportion remembered discord between their parents. Their educational attainment was generally low. Only two had stayed on at school after 16 and the majority left without any qualification. Most were unemployed when they were interviewed and had been so for the preceding year. For all these reasons the circumstances in which they were bringing up their children were fairly bleak; they were also having to cope with parenthood at a comparatively young age, on average 18 years for mothers and 22 for fathers.

The consequences for the children of social and economic adversity were clear. There were 25 boys and 18 girls between the ages of one month and 13 years. They were a wanted and normal group of babies at birth, but half the mothers reported misgivings in the months following and a fifth experienced lengthy ambivalence, which in one case bordered on rejection.

The level of injury which the children sustained was quite slight. None died and in 12 cases no specific injury was alleged. However, the psychological state of the children gave rise to serious concern. Thirty-three were rated as disturbed by the social workers, and all but five by their own mothers. The relationship between parents and the abused child was generally described favourably by social workers and aspects of care such as feeding, washing and clothing, which are easier to make allowances for in a context of financial hardship, were regarded as acceptable. On the other hand, parents tended to be markedly unresponsive to the emotional needs of their children and to spend little time with them in ways which required their active engagement. Mothers especially described failing to discipline their children consistently, resorting instead to spasmodic hitting, shouting or attempts to reason, all to little long-term or even short-term effect. Their parenting was characterised by its passivity and the patterns of control were considered erratic.

Earlier psychological research suggested that the style of parenting, whether permissive or controlling, had an effect on the sociability of the child growing up. Highly punitive and highly permissive parents tended to have highly aggressive children (Sears et al, 1957). Oldershaw, Walters and Hall (1986) considered abusing mothers to be intrusive in their interactions with the children and Trickett and Kuczyinski (1986) found the children of abusive parents to be more aggressive as reported by their parents.

In tune with certain psychological research which found an association between laxity and inconsistency in parental handling and aggressive behaviour in children, there was evidence to suggest that the nature of the daily interaction between parents and the children they were considered to have abused might inadvertently reinforce a pattern of behaviour which gave rise to mutual frustration. The less responsibility parents took for the discipline of their children, the more difficult to handle the children became.

Child Abuse Interventions: A Review of the Research Literature
David Gough, University of Glasgow

This extensive review examined the literature available up to 1992 on the effectiveness of interventions to prevent or respond to abuse. It was designed primarily as a ground-clearing exercise to inform the planning of future studies and as such had a bearing on the way the Department of Health programme was originally conceived.

One dimension of Gough's work was a look at programmes aimed at educating adults and the community about abuse. The need to develop such a strategy was found to be more pressing than the need to evaluate its effectiveness. Gough concluded that developing general parenting and child care skills and increasing awareness about the nature of child abuse and the responsibilities of child protection agencies might do much to improve the effectiveness of interventions when they are actually needed.

For sexual abuse, Gough reported that there was good empirical support for the effectiveness of preventative educational programmes for children and for some treatment services for perpetrators. In contrast, research data on the effectiveness of treatment for victims and survivors were limited. There was some support for the benefit of certain group and individual therapies, but little to suggest that one approach was superior to any other.

Among the 225 English language publications David Gough summarised, he found only a few which he felt could properly be classed as formal evaluations. The most successful were demonstration projects with very large sample groups or narrowly focused examinations of specific interventions. Many of the remainder he considered to be limited methodologically. The results from the most analytically rigorous tests of practice tended to be among the least encouraging.

His review includes detailed systematic summaries of all the 225 studies in terms of their sample, focus, objectives, methods, design measures and results. They are discussed in chapters on the education of children, adults and the community, the involvement of volunteers and parent aides, antenatal and post-natal services, adult and child groups, behavioural approaches, special projects, multi-component interventions, routine services, special initiatives and the particular difficulties associated with sexual abuse

The few existing studies of child protection practice indicated the importance of both service and case variables in predicting case outcome. Gough argued for more such studies and drew attention to the research potential of routine child abuse management information systems, which are still in their infancy in Britain. Gough found that most intervention studies concerned specialist centres with the researchers making little reference to routine services or to the legal and procedural aspects of protection work. He found, too, that most studies were weakened by their lack of reference to a wider research and practice base, for example to the development of family support programmes.

There was a need for coherence in the theoretical assumptions that different programmes employed. Other future requirements were that studies should assess the interaction between activities directed towards child protection and those concerned with therapeutic change and that both case definition and the content of the intervention should be precisely stated and controlled.

Since the whole concept of child abuse was largely based on parental responsibility for the distress of their children, he concluded, the service response was likely to be concerned with perceptions of the adequacy of the parents as carers. Yet child abuse research and sometimes child protection services were artificially separated from other research and practice concerning the support of children and families. Abuse was only one form of adverse childhood experience and only one aspect of poor parenting. It must not be artificially separated from other areas of individual and interpersonal difficulty.

The relevance of North American research on child protection

Most of the research reviewed in this Resource Book originates from the United Kingdom. Many other studies have been undertaken elsewhere, particularly in the United States where the pioneering work of the Kempes and Finkelhor has long focused on child protection. The sheer volume of this literature makes its inclusion here unrealistic, but it is possible to compare the way in which the general themes emerging in this publication are dealt with. For those requiring more information, the National Research Council report *Understanding Child Abuse and Neglect* provides a useful review.

Much of the discussion in the United States has focused on definitions of abuse. Researchers disagree about whether child maltreatment is best identified as a continuum of behaviours, ranging from absolutely safe to very dangerous (an approach not dissimilar to the concept of thresholds used in this book) or as a unique set of behavioural problems each of which has its own causes, pathways and effects. North American researchers have become increasingly interested in the process of child rearing, particularly disruptions which result from serious family problems, drug abuse and mental illness. From this perspective, abuse is said to occur when risk factors in the child's home outweigh any protective factors.

Given this focus, it is unsurprising to find that research has delved deeper into family circumstances and its effects on children's upbringing than is the case in Britain. The influence of parents' personality attributes, for example, anger or anxiety and stress factors in the home, such as marital conflict, absence of a significant adult, a difficult child, poverty and unemployment, have been carefully measured. Many studies have also emphasised the consequences of maltreatment for all family members (including the perpetrator). As in the United Kingdom, it is chronically neglecting families that are increasingly causing concern.

In the United States more attention has been given to links between child abuse, environmental factors, community characteristics and socio-cultural values. Many of the several million children subject to abuse investigations in the USA live in extreme poverty. Much debate surrounds the question of whether the over-representation of poor children is an effect of over-reporting or of living circumstances. The term 'societal neglect' has been used to describe the way in which the state's failure to support the poorest of the poor particularly disadvantages children.

The identification of child abuse was previously more sophisticated in the United States than in the United Kingdom. This may explain why a higher rate of children are the subject of abuse investigations, are removed from home or receive some other intervention. Precise comparisons are difficult but the 1.7 million reports affecting 2.7 million children indicate a referral rate at least three times that of the UK and the rate of children in state care because of maltreatment is also several times higher. It is against this background that policies, supported by research, have urged greater prevention to keep children at home; an approach known in this country as family support.

Preventative strategies are variable, both in their application and effects. Parental enhancement schemes, including health visiting (not a universal service in the USA), centre-based and community-based programmes, have been introduced. However, the aims of such initiatives are not well-defined and outcome evidence is limited. The research that is available suggests that parents can learn a lot about child development in a short period but that change in parenting style, attitudes and skills take much longer to achieve. Community-based prevention schemes, largely to reduce the effects of poverty, are also widespread. Much more work is undertaken in schools although, again, the value of these initiatives, as scientifically evaluated, is doubtful.

Compared with the Department of Health research programme, the American studies have distinct strengths and weaknesses. Over there, much more is known about the consequences of maltreatment upon children. Effects that have been investigated range from peer relationships to extreme violence although it is continually stressed that most abused children *do not* show signs of extreme disturbance. The National Research Council report emphasises the importance of the timing, intensity and context of abuse in understanding its consequences. Knowledge in this area is being taken forward by comparisons between behaviours which can be explained by childhood maltreatment and those which have other causes. A further question frequently raised asks whether victims' disorder only surfaces at times of stress.

Research on interventions and treatment for abused children is less well developed. Compared with the range of parenting programmes, preventative schemes and extensive provision under child welfare for children living away from home, there are relatively few services aimed at alleviating the psychosocial problems presented by abused children and there is little systematic evaluation of those that exist.

In conclusion, policy makers, practitioners and researchers interested in child abuse in the United States and the United Kingdom have many similar concerns. It is probably no longer true to say that other countries lag behind North American pioneers in this field as there are significant strengths and weaknesses of the different research programmes. It is important to consider the different contexts in which studies are mounted when making international comparisons and interpreting results.

For example, in the USA there is a distinction between family support services (which are usually outside the child welfare service) and family preservation services (with are usually located within it). In the United Kingdom, this division has not occurred and research on outcomes of focused interventions has, therefore, been easier to achieve.

Against this background, the USA has more cases reported (three times that for the UK) and more child abuse deaths (four times that for the UK). It also has twice as many children in state care, all of whom have been separated by court order. The United States has also mounted extensive programmes to prevent substitute care placement and research to evaluate outcomes of such schemes. Interventions, therefore, tend to display features of both *child rescue and strong prevention* (both of abuse and of substitute care placement). In the United Kingdom the emphasis is more on *child protection and family support*, wherever possible, for children living at home; here the courts have relatively little involvement in the process. These differences should be borne in mind when comparisons are drawn.

True for Us: practical exercises

Two sorts of criticism are frequently levelled at research. One is to do with timing, *What you say may have been true then, but it probably isn't now.* The other is about place, *What you say may be true there, but it probably doesn't apply here.* Such doubts make research less authoritative and lessen its impact on policy and practice.

The following practical exercises try to provide a counter to both complaints by suggesting how professionals, managers and students can translate the research findings to their own situation and so test the value of this book. It is hoped that they will be found useful not only by those who have the time and the resources to apply them in training, management or practice. They work as well as a basis for reflection on the relationship between the broad sweep of the research studies and the circumstances of individual local authorities and neighbourhoods.

Twelve exercises are provided. They can be used by individuals at any level in the child protection system, by teams of professionals, by multi-disciplinary or cross-agency groups, or as part of a training programme. They are designed to serve a variety of purposes, such as self-monitoring or evaluating services or in agency audits of skills and processes. Each exercise is concerned specifically with particular issues raised in the Overview and so can be undertaken on its own. All will help provide an answer to the question: *Is the research true for us?*

Index to Exercises

The problems of definition

1 Defining child abuse
2 Professionals' definitions of protection issues

The child protection process

3 The characteristics of child protection cases and the management of workloads
4 The child protection process: criteria for decision making
5 Family types, family services and child protection

How can professionals best protect children?

6 What happens in your local child protection system?
7 Assessing outcomes and evaluating services

How effective is the child protection process?

8 Communication with parents and carers
9 Partnership and parental participation

Conclusions

10 Incidents, context and evidence
11 The relationship between need, protection and welfare
12 The wider welfare needs of children

Some exercises are more relevant than others to the work of particular individuals and groups. Exercises 1,3,4,5,6,8,9 and 12 should interest those working directly with children and families, while 4,5,6 and 7 cover some of the concerns of ACPC members. Exercises 1,3,4,5,6,7,11 and 12 require the preparation of materials. An important issue to raise in every exercise is the potential use of the forthcoming material for policy and practice developments.

This exercise is for frontline child protection workers and their managers, working in groups or pairs.

1 Defining child abuse

Child abuse is difficult to define, yet clear parameters for intervention are required if professionals are to act with confidence to protect vulnerable children. Thresholds which legitimise action on the part of child protection agencies are the most important component of any definition of child abuse

Aim To develop the concept of a 'threshold' for defining abuse, to establish the factors that make up the threshold in various agencies and consider the consequences for children of the thresholds employed in a given set of circumstances.

Preliminary tasks Make a set of cards like the ones below. The cards should be dealt to groups who should discuss what additional information they would need to enable them to decide whether each incident could be defined as child abuse.

1	2	3	4
A girl aged six arrives in school with a bruise on the side of her face. She says she bumped into a table.	A boy in infant school says he has been watching naughty videos with his dad.	A six year old regularly comes to school without a coat, wearing threadbare jeans, a thin sweatshirt and torn trainers. He brings sweets for his lunch.	A three year old clings to the health visitor during a home visit. She wants to be held and is reluctant to return to her stepmother.

5	6	7	8
A six week old breast-fed baby of middle class parents, the third child after a gap of six years, has not regained his birth weight. Mother insists he is content and feeds well.	A girl of twelve is reported to be falling behind with school work. She is withdrawn and reluctant to join in with class activities. Her parents have recently separated.	Several bruises are noticed on the back of the legs of an eleven year old boy who is reluctant to change for PE. He says he doesn't know what caused them.	A twelve year old girl from an ethnic minority family writes in an essay that she sleeps in the same bed as her father.

1 In small groups take one of the cards as an example. As group members you should ask yourselves:
- Whether abuse may have occurred
- Why you have come to that conclusion
- Whether areas of doubt remain.

Describe the additional information you would need to be certain that this is a case of:
- Physical abuse
- Sexual abuse
- Emotional abuse
- Neglect
- Failure to thrive

2 Read pp14–18 of the Overview on Thresholds for Intervention. In relation to the case(s) you have considered is the threshold in your agency for defining abuse too high or too low; are criteria included in the threshold too wide or too narrow? Do you think this has any consequences for the children?

An exercise for a multi-disciplinary team to enable the responses of different professional groups to be compared and contrasted.

2 Professionals' definitions of protection issues

Thresholds which legitimise action on the part of child protection agencies are the most important components of any definition of child abuse. However, thresholds will be set differently by different professions and the sub-groups within them.

Aim   To attempt to analyse the threshold of child abuse from the point of view of the individual, the professional and society, to identify contrasts between professional disciplines and to consider the consequences for children of the similarities and differences.

Scenario   During PE a teacher notices a large bruise on the shin of a five-year-old child. When asked how he or she came to be hurt the child says only, 'I don't know,' and looks unhappy. It has already been observed that the child has become miserable and withdrawn and recoils when approached by adults. When the parents are asked how the child came to be bruised, they say either 'I don't know' or explain that a younger sibling kicked him or her.

Consider also these three family backgrounds:

1 The child is the eldest of three. The siblings are aged two years and ten months. Their single, young mother is receiving income support. The family are known to social services because of the youngest child's failure to thrive.

2 The child lives with his or her natural mother and her new partner. There is a three year-old child and a new baby. When collected from school by the partner, the child was reluctant to go home with him.

3 The child lives with both parents, who are married. Both used to work full-time. There is a younger sibling aged three, who has asthma and is frequently in hospital. The child has been late for school on several mornings recently and arrives screaming and pulling against his or her parent. Parents appear to be under stress and uncommunicative.

1 Discuss whether you would define any combination of circumstances as a case of suspected child abuse. Give reasons for and against your decision.

2 Depending on your decision, consider what action to take. Again give reasons.

3 Look at pp14-18 of the Overview on Thresholds for Intervention. Compare answers in the light of this analysis and decide whether similarities or differences exist between professional disciplines with respect to how and at what point thresholds are set to define abuse and so to trigger action. Are there differences/similarities in the factors that determine thresholds?
What consequence (if any) does all this have for children?
What should be done with this information; who is responsible for assessing it?

An exercise for any professional
with a substantial child
protection workload and for
those who manage them.

3 The characteristics of child protection cases and the management of workloads

The research on outcomes in child protection helps draw attention to individual cases and the way professionals manage their caseloads. It also provides a starting point for discussion during supervision and team work. Analysis of individual caseloads and the overall workload of a team can make it possible to identify good and poor outcomes and the reasons for them. This in turn can provide a basis for planning individual training needs as well as a guide to requirements for training programme developments.

Aim

To generate a caseload analysis in order to identify any general patterns in the workload of an individual or a team of professionals and to explore the reasons for them.

Preliminary tasks

You may want to consider whether this exercise is best approached as a distinct task at a particular moment or whether to review a caseload over a period of, for example, one month or three months.

1 Complete the analysis chart reproduced on the next page for each of the cases you are working on, taking account of the criteria given at the head of the columns. When the chart is complete, answers to each question should be totalled to produce aggregate figures at the foot of each column.

2 Look at the two sets of results and link them by asking:
Are certain cases better protected than others?
What are the features that make this so?
From the point of view of their general welfare, do some children improve more than others?

3 Rate each case in terms of the following outcomes:
Is the child protected?   How?
                             If not, why not?
Has the general welfare of the child been improved?
                             How?
                             If not, why not?
Have the needs of the parents/carers been met?
                             How?
                             If not, why not?
Look at the findings of Farmer and Owen, pp61-64, as they relate to the questions just answered in sections 2 and 3. Consider how similar they are to what you have found.

	Note the age of each child and use the space at the foot of the column to calculate an average age	Note the gender of the child	Is there any relationship between the gender of the abuser and the way cases are allocated?	Is there a relationship between the occupation of the abuser and the way cases are allocated?	Use the space at the foot of the column to note the number of cases by the type of abuse	Is the abuse intra or extra familial?	Say whether the decision was based on personal choice, supervisor decision or team decision
	Age of child	Gender of child	Gender of abuser	Occupation of abuser	Type of abuse	Relationship of perpetrator to victim	Method of allocation
Case 1,2 etc.							
Concerning the whole caseload	Average age of children	Proportion of boys and girls	The relationship between the gender of abusers and the way cases are allocated	The occupation of abusers	The proportion of types of abuse	The proportion of intra and extra familial abuse	The method of case allocation

4 The child protection process: criteria for decision making

For a group of inter-agency staff used to working together or a group of practitioners from a social services department. This exercise could also be carried out by ACPC members to analyse practice decisions.

Out of approximately 160,000 child protection referrals made annually to social services departments, research estimates that only 40,000 are conferenced and fewer than 25,000 lead to a name being placed on the child protection register.

Aim

This exercise seeks to establish the criteria used in your authority to process cases through the system. It will increase understanding of the different reasons professionals have for referring children to the protection services and their differing expectations of what it can achieve.

Preliminary tasks

Be familiar with page 28 and pp33-34 in the Overview and the summaries of the research by Gibbons, Conroy and Bell on pp68-70.

Data collection

Select four recently referred cases using the following criteria:
one which was referred but was not investigated,
one which was investigated but where there was a decision not to conference,
one conferenced but where a child was not registered,
one conferenced and where a child was registered.

1 Examine each of the four cases selected to decide:
What criteria were used to reach the decision?
What family needs were established in the enquiry?
What support services, if any, were offered to the family?

2 Consider your findings in the light of your agency's procedures. Compare them with the research findings concerning factors that determined which cases proceeded through different stages of the child protection system (pp33-34 of the Overview). With this knowledge, look again at the factors that apply in your area. What does a comparison with the factors identified by research indicate about your local system?

3 Review the exercise and try to answer the following questions:
- Was it easy to establish the criteria being used?
- Do your present procedures provide clear criteria for reaching decisions at each stage?
- Did the decision making process focus on the abusive activity or on the broader needs of the family?
- At what stage in the process were the family's needs defined?

Note: the research indicates the factors that were significant for decision making at the time of the study. It does not say that these should be the factors determining a child's progress through the protection system.

Finally, two key questions in the light of the research messages:
- Looking again at the four cases, could the family's needs have been defined and services offered at an earlier stage?
- Would these services have changed the extent to which the cases were involved in the child protection system?

This exercise concerns the framework of service delivery and resourcing. It can be undertaken in a day or over a number of sessions by a manager working alone, by ACPC members or frontline practitioners.

5 Family types, family services and child protection

The family circumstances of children who are subject to a Section 47 enquiry are varied but generally unhappy. Cleaver and Freeman identified five family types which help to illustrate the range of background characteristics to be borne in mind when abuse is suspected. They are: *multi-problem families, specific problem families, acutely distressed families, outside perpetrators, infiltrating perpetrators.*

Aim

To enable managers and ACPCs to use the Cleaver/Freeman typology to assess the relationship between child protection and family support work in their current service provision to families and children.

Preliminary tasks

Be familiar with the boxed paragraphs on page 20 in the Overview and the summaries of the research by Cleaver and Freeman on pp59-61.

Data collection ❶

An area manager (or ACPC) should look at all recent referrals (e.g. last two months) in which there was a protection issue.
Families should be categorised using the Cleaver/Freeman family types.
The services subsequently provided to each family should be listed.

Analysis ❷

Consider what patterns of service provision are detectable within and between the family types. Do the families of each type receive broadly similar services? Do some family types receive more services than others?
Does there appear to be a rationale for this pattern of service provision? If so, what is it? Does it take into account abusive incidents, parental needs and the availability of resources?

On reflection ❸

Could and should any of the families and children have been provided with these, or other services, without a Section 47 enquiry? Would it have been necessary for the referral to have occurred earlier? Could the response have been different without any alteration to the timing?
To which of the five categories of family do you think your agency and the ACPC might allocate referrals as 'family need' rather than 'abusive incident', so removing them from the Section 47 framework to the Section 17 framework?

If this exercise was successful you might usefully continue it by asking the following questions:

- How might your agency redefine and reorganise resources in order to meet family need?
- How would such a family support framework take proper account of minor abusive incidents?

The research suggests that where the response framework was geared to family support rather than child protection, families were likely to be more welcoming to child care workers. Where the views of workers and family members coincided and there was a sense of partnership, children appeared to do better.

- Do you agree and, if so, why?
- If a continuum of service was successfully established, and child protection and family support were brought together (without dissipating the agency's child protection skills), how might children and families benefit?

6 What happens in your local child protection system?

It emerged from the research that approximately 160,000 children and families a year are drawn into the child protection process but that the names of fewer than 25,000 children are registered. It appeared that many of the children and families would benefit from services under Section 17 of the *Children Act* 1989 and that providing services by those means would increase parental co-operation, one of the key indicators of successful intervention.

For any experienced professional.This exercise could take place as a team development activity over a number of weeks. Information could then be created as a team resource subsequently to be maintained and updated.

Aim

To encourage the use of research and monitoring information to inform and improve local policy and practice.

Preliminary tasks

Be familiar with page 28 in the Overview and summaries of the research by Gibbons, Conroy and Bell on pp68-70.

1 Ask participants if they know what type of statistical information about child protection is collected locally and nationally. Divide into pairs or small groups and set each the task of collecting information to answer one or more of the following questions:
- How many referrals are received by your agency/team each year?
- How many child abuse investigations take place each year?
- How many investigations lead to a child being removed from home?
- How many lead to Emergency Protection Orders?
- How many cases result in a child protection conference being called?
- How many lead to court proceedings?
- In how many cases was the perpetrator removed from the home?
- In how many cases were further services offered following investigation?

2 In the light of this evidence, it is important to consider whether a particular authority has a high or low conferencing and registration rate. Therefore an attempt should be made to compare results with other authorities of similar population size and characteristics. Staff in high registering authorities need to ask themselves:
- How many criteria on page 31 of the Overview apply to your authority?
- Should any action be taken to alter this?

Staff in low registering authorities need to ask themselves:
- What percentage of cases not registered are closed without further action?
- What percentage of cases which are not registered go on to be considered in a multi-agency forum to decide whether the children are in need? How many subsequently receive a service and from which agency?
- What percentage of cases investigated but not conferenced are considered in a multi-agency forum?
- How many go on to receive a service and from which agency?
- What percentage of cases conferenced but not registered receive services and from which agencies?

You will need to refer to the Department of Health publication *Children and Young People on Child Protection Registers* prepared annually by the Government Statistical Service.

A practical questionnaire designed for the members of Area Child Protection Committees.

7 Assessing outcomes and evaluating services

An important message from the research is that children benefit from services in which there is a continuum of provision connecting family support and child protection. *Working Together* requires ACPCs to collate child abuse management information, a task which is likely to benefit from the use of statistics.

Aim
To clarify what information ACPCs need to collect in order to monitor services and assess outcomes effectively.

Preliminary tasks
Be familiar with the discussion on pp41-44 of the Overview and the diagram on page 28.

Understanding the child protection process
Draw a diagram relating to your area similar to the one on page 28 and complete the figures for your ACPC area. You will need to find out:
• How many children there are in your area
• How many children are referred to the child protection system (Stage 2)
• What happens to them at Stage 3
• Is the information available? If not, which agencies need to contribute.

Monitoring protection services ❷
Consider how your local figures compare with the national figures.
• What is the significance of this?
• Could the information you have collected be a basis for planning more effective services for children at risk of abuse and their families?
• Is there provision in your area for agencies to monitor which services are provided after an abuse enquiry has been completed?
• What use do individual agencies make of the information they collect?
• Is it, or could it be supplied to the ACPC to inform service planning and quality assessment?

Planning services for protection and prevention ❸
• What circumstances motivate professionals to attend multi-agency meetings?
• How is the quality or amount of information provided by various agencies related to the services available?

Research indicates that a number of children will be re-abused.
• Which agencies already collate information about re-abuse?
• Which agencies would be in a position to do so?
• Do these include education, health, police and social services?
• Is evidence on the repetition of abuse put into the context of the following: the register status of the child; the type of abuse; the age, gender and ethnic group of the child; services provided for the family; the identity of the abuser?
• How could the information be used to plan services for the better protection of children in your area?

Although it is highlighted by many police forces as a source of increasing concern, serious marital conflict is shown by research often to be underestimated as a risk factor in children's lives.
• How can police information be made available to ACPCs to determine the extent of the problem?
• Can ACPCs use this information to plan preventative services for families?
• What is the situation with regard to other risks to children identified in the research, such as bullying at school or racial attacks?

This series of exercises has been designed for multi-disciplinary training groups and for use on DipSW courses.

8 Communication with parents and carers

The better the communication between professionals and parents, the more likely it is that the outcome for the child and family will be protective and positive. Whether or not enquiries proceed, the research shows that a great deal of anxiety is likely to require attention before a professional can communicate freely with a parent or carer.

Aim

To enable social workers and other professionals who deal with allegations of child abuse to consider their response to parents' questions during the initial stages of an investigation.

Preliminary tasks

Be familiar with pp37–39 and 45–48 in the Overview and the summaries of the research by Cleaver and Freeman, pp59–61; Farmer and Owen, pp61–64; the Oxford Team, pp79–81 and Thoburn, Lewis and Shemmings, pp85–87.

1 In a team or a small group 'brainstorm' the following :
What questions do parents ask during a child abuse investigation?
What are the questions professionals find difficult to answer?
This work is particularly important between members of a multi-disciplinary group because the responses are likely to be so diverse. Parents respond in different ways to their contact with different professional groups.
Try to ensure that the following questions, all likely to be raised by parents or carers, are included.

- Why are you here?
- Who reported me?
- Who sent you?
- Are you going to take my child away?
- What is a child protection conference - what can it do?
- What is a child protection register - what does it do?
- Who will know that my child is on the child protection register?
- What if I disagree with what you say/do - whom can I complain to?
- What are my rights?
- Can I see everything you write down about me?

The information collected during the brainstorm session can be used and developed in different ways, depending on the composition of the group. Less experienced groups should work through the exercises in order. Those who work more regularly with child protection cases may prefer to incorporate more of the research evidence.

Role play **2** Using the lists collected during the brainstorm session, divide participants into groups of three or four. Give each of the groups one of the questions raised in each of the two main categories. The groups should then draw on their own experience to enact the scenario suggested by the questions.

- One person should take the role of a parent in a case they dealt with, perhaps where they felt they handled the situation badly or were posed questions they could not answer satisfactorily.

- A second person, in the role of the professional, should try out as many different responses as come to mind.
- An observer should keep a note of the different responses and the reactions of the receiver. It may also be useful to record any non-verbal communication between 'parent' and 'professional'.

The group should then discuss the responses and record on a flip chart those they found most and least useful.

If time permits, ask each participant in turn to take the role of the parent.

This experiment with role play will enable the groups to gather more information about the enquiry process, particularly in multi-disciplinary work where the information is likely to be more diverse.

Next, call a plenary session to discuss the responses made by professionals. From the exchange of information assemble a new list of helpful responses and identify areas where more work is needed. The following questions are suggested as a basis for discussion:

- Are the questions asked usually the same?
- Do different professionals get asked different questions?
- Does non-verbal communication give a conflicting message?
- Are we using excuses or blaming other people for our actions?
- Do we have all the information parents require?
- Where can we find the information we need?

Values and assumptions It is vital that those dealing with child abuse enquiries understand their reactions to parents and do not allow their own values and assumptions about behaviour to cloud their judgement. Research stresses the importance of being able to distinguish the mixed emotions of a non-abusing parent who is faced with an allegation of abuse. With this in mind the following set of questions should be considered during a final brainstorm session or group discussion.

- What do professionals expect of a non-abusing parent or carer?
- Are they realistic?
- How is the first encounter with a parent/carer likely to affect the assessment and outcome of a case?
- How do issues of the gender of the non-abusing carer affect the outcome?
- What is the influence of the ethnic origin of either carer or professional?

A useful alternative closing session would be to use a number of short, local case scenarios. Individuals could be asked to make an assessment of each case; groups should then consider whether their judgements were appropriate and on what information they were actually based. If a professional team is involved, it may be useful to consider whether there is a 'team style' of communication with parents.

A series of exercises designed for professionals involved in any aspect of child protection. They can be done by individuals, teams or small groups on any agency-based or multi-disciplinary training course.

9 Partnership and parental participation

Partnership with parents is a vital part of child protection work, but Thoburn and colleagues found that it was difficult to achieve. In their study Farmer and Owen say of parents' attendance at case conferences, 'There seemed to be an expectation not that parents would influence the conference judgement but that they would be influenced by it.'

Aim

To explain what is meant by 'partnership' and 'participation' in relation to parents in child protection and to enable professionals to evaluate the extent of family participation in case conferencee, and the degree of partnership achieved.

Preliminary tasks

Be familiar with pp45-48 in the Overview and summaries of the research by Thoburn and colleagues, pp85-87.

1 Consider each of the features in the following list and decide the relevance each has to the work with parents in your agency, i.e. all practice work, not just conferences and meetings.

	relevant	not relevant	not sure
shared values	☐	☐	☐
a shared task or goal	☐	☐	☐
trust between partners	☐	☐	☐
negotiation of plans	☐	☐	☐
decisions made together	☐	☐	☐
sharing of information	☐	☐	☐
choice in entering partnership	☐	☐	☐
both (or all) parties contribute skills and resources	☐	☐	☐
mutual confidence that each partner can and will deliver	☐	☐	☐
equality or near equality between partners	☐	☐	☐
mechanisms for reviewing and ending partnership	☐	☐	☐
formalised framework of working relationships	☐	☐	☐

2 On a scale of 1-5 estimate how well your agency, your team and you individually work in partnership with families prior to a conference, during the assessment phase and during the helping part of the work. Consider these questions:
• What is the purpose of family members attending child protection conferences?
• Is there a unity of view among professionals?
• To what extent do you think professional views about the purpose of parental attendance enhance or detract from the families' experience of partnership?
Look at some child protection conference minutes and analyse the information to answer the following questions (use a minimum of five accounts if this is an individual exercise, 20 if it is work for a team or a training course, or the information for a whole year if a research project is being attempted):
• How many conferences were attended by both parents?
• How many by one parent only? Which parent?

- Did parents attend a) the whole conference b) part of the conference c) the conclusion only?
- Were parents invited but did not attend?
- Were parents excluded?
- Did other family members attend? Who were they?
- Were family members encouraged to bring supporters?
- What input did supporters make?
- How were family members prepared?
- By whom were they prepared?
- How were they debriefed?
- Were parents and older children asked what impact the conference decision would make on their family life?

Next, consider your findings and discuss them with others: do you feel what you have uncovered amounts to partnership?

Look again at your initial 1–5 rating. Compare your judgments with those of the others in the group.

Then answer the questions:

The researchers identify in particular child-minding, lack of transport, cost, shift work.

- What factors might make it difficult for families to attend conferences?
- What does your agency offer parents/families to help them overcome these and any other difficulties? How can matters be improved?
- How does your agency seek and take account of parents' and other family members' view of the conference process, and of their view of the degree of partnership? Does your response to these questions alter your assessment of partnership on the 1–5 scale?

3 Thoburn and colleagues in their study *Paternalism or Partnership? Family Involvement in the Child Protection Process* suggest that partnership is marked by mutual respect, rights to information, accountability, competence and value accorded to individual input. In short, each partner is seen as having something to contribute, power is shared, decisions are made jointly, roles are not only respected but backed by legal and moral rights.

Using this definition, examine the minutes of a minimum of five recent child protection conferences and assess the degree of partnership achieved, looking at:

- The components of partnership listed above
- Involvement in decision making
- Consultation about decisions
- Attendance at conference but no influence or involvement in decisions
- Non-attendance at conference.

Consider your findings or discuss them with others.

- Is this what you expected?
- Are you satisfied with your agency's performance?
- What improvements can be made?
- What do professionals need to do to change the situation?
- What needs to be in place to enable families to achieve real partnership?

This is an exercise for two or three interdisciplinary groups, each comprising two to five people.

10   Incidents, context and research evidence

The thresholds for defining child abuse and for taking action require incidents to be assessed in their context and in the light of research knowledge about what is bad for children.

Aim

To consider the relationships between a potentially abusive incident, the context in which it occurs and research evidence on what happens to children at risk and their families.

Preliminary task

Be familiar with the discussion of the complex relationship between these factors in pp14–20 of the Overview.

Each group should take at random one of the five pieces of information from each of the following three categories. (There are 125 possible combinations.)

Potentially abusive incidents

1   A child's level of interaction with his or her mother is said to be poor.
2   Fingertip bruising is noticed on a child's arm.
3   There are reports from school that a child has repeatedly exposed himself.
4   A child makes disclosures about sexual abuse.
5   A child's behaviour at school is reported to be lethargic and withdrawn.

Context

1   The child is aged three. The family are well known to social services. The mother is coping alone and there are housing problems.
2   The child is aged seven. The family have recently moved to the area and are not known to social services. The father works intermittently. Living conditions in the home are reasonably good, but the mother shows signs of depression and there are suggestions about domestic violence.
3   The child is ten. The family are known to social services although they live in very prosperous surroundings. The child has been attending child guidance clinic. Father has been receiving medication for depression.
4   The child is aged 14. There are also five younger brothers and sisters in the family, three of whom are in care or accommodation. The three children at home are looked after by their father and stepmother. Household resources, though stretched, are adequate.
5   The child is aged ten and boards at an EBD school, returning to be with his mother and stepfather or father and stepmother on alternate weekends. The family is relatively prosperous.

Research evidence

1   Families drawn into the child protection process are, in the main, multiply disadvantaged, a characteristic not always found in the wider population of abused children. Nearly all children (96%) remain at home and the majority of those separated are swiftly reunited.
2   Child protection enquiries seek not only to establish whether maltreatment has occurred but to gauge whether the family can benefit from support services. Too frequently, enquiries become investigations and, in over half of cases, families receive no services at all in the aftermath of the professionals' interest in their lives.

3 The child protection process has the capacity to direct a wide range of services towards children in need. If they are not deployed with proper care, there is a danger that they may overwhelm those they are meant to help or too severely circumscribe parental responsibility and autonomy.

4 Many children in need live in contexts in which their health and development are neglected. In these cases it is the corrosiveness of long-term emotional, physical and occasional sexual maltreatment that causes psychological impairment or even significant harm.

5 The conclusion that between a quarter and a third of children who have been in contact with the child protection process are re-abused is disquieting. Concern is tempered somewhat by the low incidence of severe maltreatment.

1 The group should consider whether there is any connection between the three pieces of information they have selected. Does such a perception help to determine what services should be provided and which procedures followed?

2 Each group should then report its findings to the rest.

3 Repeat the exercise with different selections of incidents, contexts and research evidence.

For team leaders meeting as a group or team leaders and their staff.

11 The relationship between need, protection and welfare

The research shows that agencies involved in child protection are often too remote from family support services, each having their own staff, ways of working and resources. Since the problems faced by children and families are complex, practical benefits can come from an approach which merges questions about the child's protection with others about support for the family.

Aim

To clarify the relationship between need, protection and welfare by closely examining cases.

Preliminary tasks

Be familiar with pp53–56 in the Overview. It may be helpful for the group undertaking the task to split into pairs to look at the cases and to regroup to discuss findings.

Data collection

Choose four cases currently being offered family support services via a family centre or other support facilities, such as day care, family aide, homestart, etc.

1 Examine each case in detail and decide:
- Who sought the services and for what reasons?
- What criteria were used to decide whether the family should be offered a service?
- What family needs were established?
- What was the intended outcome of the package of support being offered?
- Are there child protection issues in these families?

Data collection

Choose four cases currently the subject of a child protection plan.
Repeat the process described in Step One and compare the results with your analysis of the family support service cases.

2 Look at the two sets of answers and consider:
- What are the similarities within the two groups, i.e. those offered family support services and those the subject of a child protection plan, in terms of the needs established and services offered?
- How do the criteria differ?
- How do the established needs differ?
- How do the services provided differ?

Do you think that a continuum of services as described on page 56 would provide a better framework for these cases?

An exercise suitable for any professional involved in child protection work.

12 The wider welfare needs of children

Farmer and Owen's study showed that the wider needs of 32% of the children who were the subject of a protection conference were not adequately dealt with. This finding is echoed in several other studies, such as those by Cleaver, Sharland, Thoburn and colleagues.

Aim

To compare the child's needs as identified in comprehensive social work assessments with those addressed in protection plans and accompanying services.

Preliminary tasks

Be familiar with pp47-48 in the Overview and summaries of the research by Farmer and Owen, pp61-64 and, if time allows, Cleaver and Freeman, pp59-61; Sharland and colleagues, pp79-81 and Thoburn and colleagues, pp85-87. Select a number of cases which have recently been the subject of a child protection plan. Have the file papers available for inspection.

Option ❶

Examine an assessment or review form for each case selected, identify any needs in the following seven areas of the child's life and draw up a list in a similar form to the diagram.

Needs

Health

[ ]

Education

[ ]

Identity

[ ]

Family relationships

[ ]

Social presentation

[ ]

Emotional and behavioural development

[ ]

Self-care skills

[ ]

Option **2** To do the exercise more comprehensively, the *Looking After Children* materials published by the Department of Health should be applied. Copies may be available from the local authority social services department or they can be obtained beforehand from HMSO. The materials consist of age appropriate Assessment and Action Records covering seven areas of children's lives listed above. Training materials are also available.

3 Select one or preferably more cases that have been the subject of a child protection conference. Examine the background material made available to the conference and additional material recorded in social work files and assessments. From these, identify the needs of the child as follows:
- Child protection needs
- Other needs which would benefit from services
- Other needs beyond the reach of services.

Apply the framework above or the *Looking After Children* schedule appropriate to the child. From these, repeat the previous exercises by identifying the needs of the child, as follows:
- Child protection needs
- Other needs which would benefit from services
- Other needs beyond the reach of services.

Compare the two assessments of need:
- Is there any difference?
- Are these differences important?
- What needs to be done to meet the unmet need identified?

Bibliography

Audit Commission, *Seen but not Heard: Co-ordinating Community Child Health and Social Services for Children in Need*, HMSO, 1994.

Baker, A. and Duncan, S., 'Child sexual abuse: a study of prevalence in Britain', *Child Abuse and Neglect*, 9, 457-467, 1985.

Birchall, E. and Hallett, C., *Working Together in Child Protection*, HMSO, 1995.

Browne, K. and Saqi, S., 'Parent-child interaction in abusing families and its possible causes and consequences' in Maher, P. (ed.), *Child Abuse: The Educational Perspective*, Basil Blackwell, pp77-104, 1987.

Bullock, R., Little, M. and Millham S., *Going Home*, Dartmouth, 1993.

Cleaver, H. and Freeman, P., *Parental Perspectives in Cases of Suspected Child Abuse*, HMSO,1995.

Clyde, J., *The Report of the Inquiry into the Removal of Children from Orkney in February 1991*, HMSO, 1992.

Davies, C., 'An overview of research on children' in *DH Yearbook of Research and Development*, pp.35-39, HMSO, 1990.

Department of Health and Social Security, *Social Work Decisions in Child Care: Recent Research Findings and their Implications*, HMSO, 1985.

Department of Health, *Protecting Children, A Guide for Social Workers Undertaking a Comprehensive Assessment*, HMSO, 1988.

Department of Health, *Patterns and Outcomes in Child Placement: Messages from Current Research and their Implications*, HMSO, 1991.

Dingwall, R., Eekelaar, J. and Murray, T., *The Protection of Children*, Basil Blackwell, 1983.

Family Rights Group, *The Children Act 1989: Working in Partnership with Families, Reader,* HMSO, 1991.

Farmer, E. and Owen, M., *Child Protection Practice: Private Risks and Public Remedies - Decision Making, Intervention and Outcome in Child Protection Work*, HMSO, 1995.

Finkelhor, D. and Hotaling, G. 'Sexual abuse in the national incidence study of child abuse and neglect: An appraisal' *Child Abuse and Neglect*, 8, 23-32, 1984.

Finkelhor, D., *A Sourcebook on Child Sexual Abuse*, Sage, 1986.

Gallagher B., Parker H. and Hughes, B. *Organised and Ritual Child Sexual Abuse* Report to ESRC, University of Manchester, 1994.

Ghate D. and Spencer, L., *The Prevalence of Child Sexual Abuse in Britain: A Feasibility Study for a Large Scale National Survey of the General Population*, HMSO, 1995.

Giarretto, H., 'A comprehensive child sexual abuse treatment program', *Child Abuse and Neglect*, 6, 263-278, 1982.

Gibbons, J., Gallagher, B., Bell, C. and Gordon, D., *Development After Physical Abuse in Early Childhood: A Follow-Up Study of Children on Protection Registers,* HMSO, 1995.

Gibbons, J., Conroy, S. and Bell, C.,*Operating the Child Protection System: A Study of Child Protection Practices in English Local Authorities*, HMSO, 1995.

Gil, D., *Violence Against Children*, Harvard University Press, 1970.

Gough, D., *Child Abuse Interventions: A Review of the Research Literature*, HMSO, 1993.

Gough, D., Boddy, F., Dunning, N. and Stone, F. *The Management of Child Abuse: A Longitudinal Study of Child Abuse in Glasgow*, Scottish Office, Central Research Unit Papers, 1993.

Hallett, C. *Inter-Agency Coordination in Child Protection*, HMSO, 1995.

Hallett, C., and Birchall, E., *Coordination and Child Protection*, HMSO, 1992.

HMSO, *Report of the Inquiry into Child Abuse in Cleveland 1987*, Cm 412, 1988.

Hobbs, C., Hanks, H. and Wynne, J., *Child Abuse and Neglect: A Clinician's Handbook*, Churchill Livingstone, 1993.

Home Office, Department of Health, Department of Education and Science and Welsh Office, *Working Together Under The Children Act, 1989: A Guide to Arrangements for Inter-Agency Co-operation for the Protection of Children from Abuse*, HMSO, 1991.

Kelly, L., Regan, L. and Burton, S., *An Exploratory Study of the Prevalence of Sexual Abuse in a Sample of 16-21 Year Olds*, Child and Woman Abuse Studies Unit, University of North London, 1991.

Kempe, R., and Kempe C., *Child Abuse*, Fontana/Open Books, 1978.

Kempe, C., Silverman, F., Steele, B., Droegmueller, W. and Silver, H., 'The battered child syndrome', *Journal of the American Medical Association*, 181, 4-11, 1962.

La Fontaine, J., *The Extent and Nature of Organised and Ritual Sexual Abuse: Research Findings*, HMSO, 1994.

Little, M. and Gibbons, J., 'Predicting the rate of children on the child protection register', *Research, Policy and Planning*, 10, 15-18, 1993.

Monck, E. and New, M., *Sexually Abused Children and Adolescents and Young Perpetrators of Sexual Abuse who were Treated in Voluntary Community Facilities*, HMSO, 1995.

Monck, E., Sharland, E., Bentovim, A., Goodall, G., Hyde, C. and Lwin, R., *Child Sexual Abuse: A Descriptive and Treatment Study*, HMSO, 1995.

Morgan, R., and Barker, M., *Sex Offenders: An Evaluation of Community Based Treatment*, Home Office Research Unit, 1993.

Mrazek P., Lynch M. and Bentovim, A., 'Sexual abuse of children in the United Kingdom', *Child Abuse and Neglect*, 6, 263-278, 1983.

National Research Council, *Understanding Child Abuse and Neglect*, National Academy Press, USA, 1993.

Newson, J. and Newson, E., *Patterns of Infant Care*, Penguin, 1969; *Four Years Old in an Urban Community*, George Allen and Unwin, 1976; *Seven Years Old In The Home Environment*, George Allen and Unwin, 1989; *The Extent of Parental Physical Punishment in the UK*, APPROACH, 1989.

Oldershaw, L., Walters, G. and Hall, D., 'Control strategies and non-compliance in abusive mother-child dyads: an observational study', *Child Development*, 57, 722-732, 1986.

Parker, R., Ward, H., Jackson, S., Aldgate, J., and Wedge, P. (eds.), *Looking After Children: Assessing Outcomes in Child Care*, HMSO, 1991.

Schechter, M. and Roberge, L., 'Sexual exploitation' in Helfer, R. and Kempe, C. (eds.), *Child Abuse and Neglect*, Balinger, pp127-142, 1976.

Sears, R., Maccoby E. and Levin, H., *Patterns of Child Rearing*, Harper and Row, 1957

Sharland E., Jones, D., Aldgate, J., Seal, H. and Croucher, M., *Professional Intervention in Child Sexual Abuse*, HMSO, 1995.

Skuse, D. and Bentovim, A., 'Physical and emotional maltreatment' in Rutter, M., Taylor, E. and Hersov, L. (eds.), *Child and Adolescent Psychiatry: Modern Approaches*, Blackwell Scientific Publications, pp209-229, 1994.

Smith, M. and Bentovim, A., 'Sexual abuse' in Rutter, M., Taylor, E. and Hersov, L. (eds.), *Child and Adolescent Psychiatry: Modern Approaches*, Blackwell Scientific Publications, pp230-251, 1994.

Smith, M. and Grocke, M., *Normal Family Sexuality and Sexual Knowledge in Children*, Royal College of Psychiatrists/Gorkill Press, 1995.

Smith, M., Bee, P., Heverin, A. and Nobes, G., *Parental Control within the Family: The Nature and Extent of Parental Violence to Children*, papers forthcoming from Thomas Coram Research Unit, Tel. 0171-612-6957.

Straus, M., Gelles, R. and Steinmetz, S., *Behind Closed Doors: Violence in the American Family*, Anchor/Doubleday, 1980.

Straus, M. and Gelles, R., 'Change in family violence from 1975 to 1985', *Journal of Marriage and the Family*, 48, 465-479, 1986.

The Research Team (Queen's University, Belfast), *Child Sexual Abuse in Northern Ireland: A Research Study of Incidence*, Greystone, 1990.

Thoburn, J., Lewis, A. and Shemmings, D., *Paternalism or Partnership? Family Involvement in the Child Protection Process*, HMSO, 1995.

Trickett, P. and Kuczyinski, L., 'Children's misbehaviours and parental discipline: strategies in abusive and non-abusive families', *Developmental Psychology*, 22, 115-123, 1986.

Waterhouse, L., Pitcairn, T., McGhee, J., Secker, J. and Sullivan, C., 'Evaluating Parenting in Child Physical Abuse' in Waterhouse, L. *Child Abuse and Child Abusers*, Jessica Kingsley, 1993.

Printed in the UK for HMSO
Dd 300662 C310 6/95